UPROOTED

A MEMOIR: SURVIVING BRITISH INDIA

ROBIN PODDER

CONTENTS

Published by: Global Publishers
Torrance, California, USA

Print ISBN: 9781088133507

Dear Nayan,

Your curiosity, innocence, and love for me have brought new meaning to my life, and I am so proud to share my story with you. Your presence in my life has been a source of constant joy and happiness.

I dedicate this memoir to you, my dear grandson, as a testament to your love and affection. Your influence on my life will stay with me forever.

ACKNOWLEDGMENTS

I am filled with gratitude, mixed with sadness, for the family members who are no longer with us. My father, mother, Borda Santosh, and Chorda Ramen were all integral parts of my memories, and I am forever grateful for the love and support they provided throughout my life. Their wisdom, strength, compassion, and generosity have been a constant source of inspiration to me, and I am so grateful for the memories we created together.

I am grateful for my sisters, Didi and Bina, who currently reside in India. I'm grateful for all the sweet memories I have with them, both in the village and in Kolkata. They will be thrilled to learn that I have finally shared my memoir with the world.

To my wife Pratima, thank you for your unwavering love and support. Your patience and understanding have been a source of comfort and strength, and I am so grateful for the life we have built together.

To my son Rahul and my daughter Ruma, thank you for the love and memories we have shared together. This memoir is a testament to that love.

I sincerely acknowledge Darren Rector, Tathagata Dasgupta, Michael Carlile, Miori Foster, Saheli Banerjee, and Mila Dasgupta and express my heartfelt gratitude for their role in this memoir. Their expertise in reading and commenting has been invaluable, and I am so thankful for the time and energy they have dedicated to this project.

As I reflect on the journey of writing this memoir, I am grateful for the support and guidance that Alicia Snyder has provided. Her expertise in editing and structuring this project has been invaluable. Her passion for perfection has helped bring my memories to life, and I cannot thank her enough for her contributions.

PREFACE

AUGUST 2019

Through a haze of half-consciousness, I felt a soothing light falling over me. I sensed the mild touch of a small, tender hand on my forehead. Through fluttering eyelids, I glimpsed my grandson Nayan standing beside my bed, touching my forehead.

"Dadu. I'm channelizing my energy to you," he said. "Soon you will feel a lot better."

"Really."

"I'm six years old now. Mamu said I can do telepathy," said Nayan.

My son, Nayan's Mamu (uncle), nodded. My daughter appeared amazed by her son Nayan's power of imagination.

Little by little, the reality sunk in: I'm lying on a hospital bed in Torrance Memorial hospital in Los Angeles. I just came out of intensive care. Last night I had an angioplasty. Two of my arteries were ninety percent clogged and they ended up inserting two stents.

At my bedside, I saw my wife, Pratima. She and my

close friends were standing around me. In addition to my family, I saw a room full of community members, mostly Bengalis. They brought flowers and Get-Well cards. They wished me a prompt recovery.

Deep inside my heart, I felt good. "Over the years, I must have contributed something to my community," I thought. "Now, I am getting rewarded for my services." I felt eternal peace as I held the hand of my grandson Nayan.

At that moment, I realized that I got my life back for a reason. As I recovered, I promised myself that every single day from now on would be used for my family and for my community. I would give every moment to enrich others' lives. And one of the ways I would do that would be by sharing my experiences in a book.

My dear Nayan, I came back from the brink of death so I could share with you the hardships I went through and the triumphs I experienced. I want you to know about the beauty of my Bengali village, the pain of being torn out of it as a young child, and the lessons I learned about overcoming adversity. I want to share my stories of heartbreak and triumph.

Nayan, I want you to know that whatever resistance you face, your perseverance and a little luck will take you to your destination.

"If they answer not to thy call, walk alone"

— *RABINDRANATH TAGORE*

PART I

BLOSSOMING: A VILLAGE BOY

PROLOGUE

The day before we left the village forever, a storm raced down the road in the center of town. Vicious and biting, it ripped through the Bengali community where I grew up. My only home.

Lightning cracked in the sky. The tall, carved posts of our mahogany bed frame stood ghastly tall in the fierce glow. I gripped the hand-embroidered bed covers spread over my mother and me. I knew it would be my last night in my bedroom, forever.

The bed I was lying on was a Chippendale, a remnant of the colonial British empire. The Indian Independence movement had recently forced our colonial rulers out of our country. But in the process of leaving, the British had caused the fierce religious conflicts that were driving us from our home. Despite the political turmoil that was beyond my control, the British bed felt warm and safe, and I drifted off to sleep once more.

When dawn came, I crept out of my room and into the

humid dawn. Outside our home, one of our mango trees lay on its side. Its bare roots stretched toward the sky like fingers. All by myself, I climbed over the broken branches to a spot where a wealth of ripe yellow mangoes lay on the ground. I picked my way through the mud and shattered twigs and gathered up as many as I could. I wrapped them in my *gamcha,* a long plaid piece of cloth that served as a scarf, a towel, or a basket.

But then a lump formed in my throat.

I won't be able to eat these with my friend Panu. I cannot take these with me. We are leaving. Today. And never coming back.

In a daze, I wandered to the back veranda of our outbuilding where my Muslim caretaker had lived in a small corner of the building. I gazed toward the kitchen where my Hindu grandmother had prepared her special vegetarian food. Now, Muslims and Hindus were being forced apart, each to their own homeland.

I stared out over the rice fields with empty eyes. Gone were the days of filling my *gamcha* with mangoes, then cracking them open with friends in the sizzling heat of summer. Gone were the innocent evenings of playing in the pond or eagerly re-enacting the great ballads of our Hindu faith. Today, I was being uprooted from my only home by a storm of division, fear, and senseless killings.

"I have to leave this forever?" I said to myself. "How will I survive?"

My very sense of self was being uprooted. My innocent childhood faith was in shambles. How would I find the strength and courage to grow again?

1

TRANQUILITY

It has been over eighty years since I left my East Bengal village, yet I can still see it in my mind's eye.

I see the gentle ripples of the pool in the center of the village, awash with gold in the setting sun.

I see the dreamy fronds of the date palm tree, waving over rich clusters of golden dates.

And I see the magnificent round flowers of the Kadamba tree: bright yellow-gold spheres, swarming like huge yellow bumblebees among the waxy green leaves, dancing like a Baul folk singer cheering the end of another day. And far across the lake, I see a mango grove extending from one corner of the pond to the other, radiating the warm, luscious scent of pure, golden sweetness.

Looking back, I can see how my entire childhood seemed to sparkle like gold. At the time, every part of my Bengali life seemed beautiful. All day long, I could see the delicate blades of rice dancing in the wind in the vast fields surrounding our home. I could see the dazzling sunshine lighting up the sky as I roamed the village unsupervised, joyful, and free. Then at dusk, I could see the warm kerosine lantern flickering across Mom's face as she and Grandma told evening stories.

Yet the things that I couldn't see were the things that were silently stalking my well-being and peace. I couldn't see the brutality and disgust that some of our traditions entailed. I couldn't see the fear that was subconsciously sinking into my mind from the stories I was told. And I was completely unaware of the conflict and upheaval that was just around the corner.

My story begins with beautiful fragments of memory which join together to create a rich, sparkling kaleidoscope of incidents, each one its own moving picture of joy. These incidents paint an image of the life of peace and tranquility we enjoyed in our once-unified village. And how that illusion was shattered beyond repair.

During its golden days, my village of Sagarkandi, Pabna was an idyllic place of peace, tranquility, and self-sustaining unity. Hindus and Muslims lived together in peace. At that time, none of us saw the tension coming between Hindus and Muslims. My family was Hindu, yet one of my dearest caregivers was a Muslim. Our Muslim household helper, Kantu Bhai, lived with our family on our large parcel of land, in one of the detached rooms scattered all across our property.

Under the supervision of my maternal uncle, Jyoti Mama, Kantu Bhai completed all sorts of errands for our family. Kantu Bhai always wore a lungi, a multicolored men's skirt, and a colorful woven towel called a *gamcha* around his waist. He had deep black hair and sharp brown eyes. His body was thin but strong, chiseled and tanned.

I knew that Kantu Bhai was Muslim. Once in a while, he used to go to the Masjid near the village bazaar. Yet that made no difference to me. He was my friend, the caregiver I looked up to. All day long, while my mother and aunt were busy in the kitchen and I was still too young to go to school, I watched Kantu Bhai stack paddy hay, cut and chop dead trees for firewood, and climb trees to fetch mangoes, guava, black Jamun, and other fruits and vegetables.

Kantu Bhai also had the responsibility of babysitting me as needed. Mother was often busy, and I felt lonely and neglected. My mom, my aunt Mamima, and my grandmother would work in the kitchen and in the bedroom from dawn to dusk. While my mother was busy, I grew profoundly bored, wishing for a playmate. My older sister, Gita, was in school, and my little sister, Gayatri, had died when she was one year old. No one else lived on our complex except my mom, grandma, aunt and uncle, and Kantu Bhai. The complex was mostly quiet except for a bird chirping or a cow moaning.

I was too young to go to school. The only way to get to school was by walking on my own two feet, and I was too young to walk down the dirt road to the school building. So I would stay at home and watch my grandmother and my mother working in and around our house, taking care of our living quarters and cleaning and cooking in the kitchen. But it got boring, so I would go outside and watch Jyoti Mama and Kantu Bhai take care of all the outdoor chores.

One day when I was four years old, I vividly remember

feeling neglected. I began to cry loudly to get my mother's attention.

"Can you take Gopal for a stroll?" my mother asked Kantu Bhai. My name is Robin, but my family called me Gopal. "See, I'm busy and he is throwing a fit."

"Yes, I will take him for a walk around the neighborhood," Kantu Bhai said.

"Make sure he does not eat too many sweets. He had a bad belly ache last night."

"I will make sure." Kantu nodded. He swooped me up onto his shoulders, which was his usual method of carrying me around. We walked out the kitchen door and sauntered past the many outbuildings and dwellings scattered across our large parcel of land. To the left, across the yard, I could see the outbuilding where Kantu Bhai lived in one corner. Once, I had asked my mother why Kantu Bhai did not live with us in the house. She said, "Kantu is from a different tribe. He is a Muslim. No Muslims or lower castes are allowed to come inside our living quarters or in our kitchen."

"Why not?"

"That's how it is."

"What is the lower caste?" I asked my mother.

"You will know when you grow up."

Though I understood that my family was Hindu, I did not understand the difference between the upper caste and lower caste. And none of it made any difference to me as Kantu Bhai and I walked off our property and turned right on the dirt path that led to our relatives' house. I was just happy he was spending time with me, giving me one-on-one attention.

Next to our house was the property of one of my uncles, Jathamosai Anathbandhu, which had been inherited from my grandfather and his brothers who had all died before I was born. Anathbandhu was probably in his mid-forties. He was a short, chubby, fair-skinned man. He was mostly bald. However, he allowed the few hairs he had left on the sides of his head to grow long, and then he carefully combed them to cover the bald part.

Anathbandhu was a pious man. Most of the time, as I recall, he would be in his worship room next to his sleeping room, chanting mantras in a sweet, melodic rhythm. Today, I knew he must have already taken a bath in the pond. That was his normal routine. He believed going into the worship room without taking a bath was a sin, as mandated by his religion.

As Kantu Bhai and I were walking past Anathbandhu's house, my uncle was standing on the veranda.

"Watch out, Kantu. Don't touch anything."

Kantu nodded and assured him that he would not touch anything. He was very much aware of the village customs. Muslims were not supposed to touch anything sacred.

We proceeded to the next neighbor's house. This was where Panu lived. Panu was my cousin's son and my dearest friend. He was about two years older than me. As Kantu Bhai entered the yard, he dismounted me and placed me on the ground. Panu's father, Suresh Da, walked out and hugged me.

"Want some sweets?" Suresh Da asked. It was the

typical village custom to offer homemade sweets, especially to a young kid.

I nodded yes. I loved to eat anything sweet! And I knew my mother was not there.

"No, no. Mother told me not to let him eat sweets," uttered Kantu Bhai, dampening my enthusiasm.

Panu came and hugged me tightly.

"Want to play marbles?" he invited. He pulled out a bunch of marbles and pointed at them. "See how shiny they are!"

"How did you get them that shiny?"

"Ambuli leaves. They have a greenish juice that cleans all glass and white marbles."

We played for a while, while Suresh Da was engaged in conversation with Kantu Bhai. After a while, Kantu Bhai picked me up and took me to the next house. There were two houses on that parcel for two of my male cousins, Gnan Da, and Dwijen Da.

As we approached their yard, we saw that Gnan Da was sitting on the veranda eating puffed rice and keeping an eye on his kids. Dwijen Da was relaxing outside, also watching his sons and daughters. Two of the kids, Govinda and Dilip, were my age. The other two were much younger. As I was playing with Govinda and Dilip, I noticed that their fathers occasionally checked on them. Suddenly, something came to my mind that I had never thought of before.

"All these kids have fathers. And I don't have one. Why?" I sat there in confusion for a moment.

When I came back to our house, Kantu Bhai dismounted me onto the floor. My mother was in the kitchen preparing food for lunch. Normally, the lunch in the village would be at noon, "after the sun hits the moon." I walked into the kitchen and asked my mother, "Mother, everybody has a father. Where is my father? Do I have a father?"

She was silent for a while. Then she said, "Baba Gopal, your father lives in Kolkata. He is not like your other relatives. They only went to school in Sagarkandi until sixth grade, and now they goof around and never set foot outside the village. But your father is a lawyer in Kolkata. He went to high school, then college, and then to university. He comes home once or twice a year. You are too young to remember that. Anyway, he may come home during Durga Puja." Durga Puja was a yearly holiday that was coming up.

"This Durga Puja?"

"Yes," she said. "Now you go, I don't have time to talk with you."

I realized this was not the right time to bother her. Things were scattered all around the clay kitchen floor. The vegetables were stacked in four or five brass containers. One container was filled with fish that had been cut, washed, and cleaned. On the wood-fire pit, I saw an iron wok. She was cooking split pea dhal. A bunch of copper spice containers were lying around. On the veranda, Mamima was preparing a wet paste of selected spices.

On the other side of the kitchen, there were two long wall-to-wall shelves scattered with brass plates, glasses, and metal containers with different condiments and legumes.

Mother looked at me and asked why I was still there. I anticipated she would spank me if I did not move. So I obeyed and stepped out.

The day went by. The daily chores were winding down, and the sun was sinking behind the horizon. As dusk crept over our quiet village, Grandma picked up her rolled mat and spread it on the bedroom veranda. She sat down and relaxed, closing her eyes. For a moment, I sat beside her, gazing up into her weathered face. A part of her nose and forehead were painted with white sandalwood paste, the special symbol of Vaishnav worshippers. She was a beautiful woman in her sixties, short and slender with a slightly elongated face. When she smiled, I noticed her staggered teeth. A couple of them were also missing. That made her smile distinct. She was always cheerful, and her touch was contagious.

Grandma wore a white dhoti and no jewelry. Since she was a widow, she was not allowed to wear colored sari, garments or any ornaments. Now, as Grandma sat beside me with her eyes closed, I mimicked her. In her hands, she held her small chanting bag with rosary beads tucked inside. Her skillful fingers slowly glided over the beads and counted one bead at a time. These were her regular morning and evening rituals. She pulled my hand gently and tugged me into her lap. I knew she was now ready to start telling a new story.

She kissed my forehead and said, "Why do you have to bother your ma when she is so busy? Ask me what you want to know."

"I just want to know why my father does not live here. Where is he?"

My grandma replied, "Your father works in Kolkata. He is a very educated man. I'm not educated enough to even be able to explain how educated he is. Everyone says that he is the most educated man in the whole district."

I asked grandma, "How long is it going to take for me to get educated like him? Will I then be able to live in Kolkata with him?"

"Sure you will," answered my grandma.

Then she told me something that I would never forget in my life. She told me that after studying for years and years, my dad had become a famous lawyer.

"What is famous?"

Grandma smiled and said, "How do I know? It was a long time ago. One day, the headmaster, Radharaman Babu, dropped by and told your grandfather that Brojen, your father, had received the highest degree from Kolkata University. He was the only boy in the entire Pabna district who passed his master's degree in English and got his degree in law, too.

Your grandfather and I did not comprehend the details of what he said. Of course, we understood your father was special.

A few months later, your father came to see us. "Do you know what happened then?" Grandma asked.

I shook my head no.

Grandma continued, "A crowd from nearby villages poured in. Lots of people. Nobody had ever seen such an educated man. The rumor started spreading. For two days, people were pouring in. They could not believe that an ordinary village boy gained such an education, competing with white sahib students."

"Tell me more, Grandma."

"That's enough for one night. It's gotten dark, and it's supper time. Let's go get the lanterns. I'll tell you the rest tomorrow."

Since that day, I have wanted to be like my father. I determined right then and there that I would one day leave the village. I would become educated, like my father.

2

THE MYSTERIES OF CHILDHOOD

That day, my grandma ignited my love for education. But the day when I could start school was still far away. For now, I had to study at home with my aunt Mamima. She helped me memorize both the Bengali and English alphabets and numbers. The rest of the day, I watched Kantu Bhai and Jyoti Mama do chores around the house. Jyoti Mama was my maternal uncle, and we used to call him "Mama," which meant "uncle." Mama was a slender man in his thirties, with a sculpted body that reflected his regular hard manual work. His body seemed to be sculpted from ebony wood. Except in winter, which only lasted a couple of months, he was always bare-bodied, wearing a short *dhoti*. Like most of the village men, he had a *gamcha* tied around his waist.

He used to take our cows out to the pasture for grazing, bring them home at sunset, and make sure that the feed supply was properly replenished. When needed, he would get a bundle of hay from the haystack and chop it to size for cattle feed. He was an indispensable handyman and my de facto guardian. Besides that, he would supervise all the errands necessary for the day-to-day upkeep and maintenance of our residence.

One day when I was four years old, I noticed that my uncle Jyoti Mama was building a very tiny shack-like structure in a space about ten feet wide in between our old and new houses. The tiny, flimsy enclosure had a slanted roof and was built with the jute sticks that we normally stored for fire starters for wood-burning pits. I watched how skillfully he put together the sides and the roof, using only jute sticks, bamboo slats, and rope. He even made a small door for the hut.

Mama noticed my curious looks and smiled.

"A brand-new brother or sister is coming soon," Mama said.

"When?" I said.

"Any moment, maybe tomorrow."

"But it looks shaky. What if it crumbles?"

Mama assured me that would never happen. After checking the strength of his construction, he started digging a trench all around the walls of the hut.

"Even if it rains, the water will never go inside."

In the meantime, his wife, my aunt Mamima, appeared at the doorway. She embraced me tightly to her chest and muttered, "Don't be scared. Your mother will be safe. Everyone gives birth the same way, and this is not her first time." She looked at Mama and asked, "Did you inform the midwife?"

"Yes, but she is out working in the field now. Don't

worry, I also asked her to make a brand-new knife from the bamboo slat and clean it properly," Mama said.

"Make sure of that."

With Mamima's reassurance, I felt much better. I fully trusted her. She was always kind and was a great helping hand to my mother. She spent a lot of time in the kitchen, expertly holding and cutting the fish that my Jyoti Mama would bring from the market.

The next morning, I woke up to urinate. Mamima, who was sleeping next to me, stood up and gave me a big hug.

"Your mother gave birth to a girl, your sister," she said.

I was elated. I slammed open the door and rushed outside. As I stepped down to see my new sister inside the hut, Mamima took hold of my hand and stopped me.

"Don't go there," she said. "If you touch that door, I will have to drag you to the well and make you take a bath."

I asked, "Why?"

She said, "The hut is untouchable. Not pure. When your mother comes out of that and moves into the house, we will burn this hut down so that there'll be no impurities. Understand?"

I did not understand, but I was told that it was part of the village customs. It was very important not to touch that shed —more important than life itself. One day during my childhood, I heard that in the next village, there was a mother who gave birth to a newborn child. As was the custom, nobody was with the mother when she gave birth, except the untrained midwife. Midwives were often married to poor peasants, and they delivered babies as a part-time business.

No money was exchanged; instead, the family gave the midwife some food on the barter system.

This mother delivered during the winter, and to keep her warm, they put a charcoal container inside her delivery room. The midwife went into the untouchable shack, delivered the baby, and went away without touching any person or any part of the main house.

After she left, the charcoal continued to burn, and eventually, the shack caught fire. Because of the superstition that the little birthplace was unsanitary and untouchable, the family who lived in the main household wouldn't even give the onlooking villagers a small hatchet to pry the burning door open.

"If you touch that house with the hatchet, the hatchet will be untouchable," the family objected.

While the villagers were discussing this and deciding what to do, the mother and child died. Touching the door, or even using a hatchet to pry it off, were both unacceptable in social norms.

The fire was not the only reason that babies died. Midwives used slitted bamboo poles to cut the babies' cords. In many cases, these unsanitary tools created sepsis, and the babies would die. There was an unbelievable death rate during childbirth in India. Of my father and mother's ten children, five of them died as children, three at birth and two when they were toddlers. But this new baby sister, my mother's tenth child, was born healthy and strong. After the time of purification was over, my mother brought little Bina out of the tiny makeshift hut.

As my parents' eighth child and youngest son, I had two

elder brothers and one older sister. Gayatri, my sister who was born right after I was, died when she was around one year old. My mother had gotten pregnant with Bina shortly after Gayatri's death, and Bina's birth was cause for great rejoicing.

"All the village elders agree that your dead sister, Gayatri, has been reincarnated as Bina!" my grandmother told me joyfully.

"Bina is a fragile and precious gift," my mother agreed, gently stroking the baby's rich, dark hair. Almost in a whisper, she added, "We must protect her."

Because of this deep-rooted belief in reincarnation, and because she was the youngest, Bina was always under constant vigilance. As she grew, she was the center of attention in our family. And the more I thought about Bina's birth, the more I wondered about my own birth.

"I will ask my mother to tell me the story of my birth," I decided one day.

Mother was extremely busy all day long, especially now that she had a new baby. She would wake up at the crack of dawn to give instructions to the helping hands and to busy herself with housework. But after sunset, she had time to sit down with us children and tell stories. On winter evenings, the sun went down early, and the kerosene lamps were lit.

The smell of kerosene lamps mingled with the scent of Grandmother's fragrant incense. She had a little pot with a charcoal fire inside, into which she poured a mixture of sulfur. The pot began to smoke with a very distinct fragrance. The smell of incense is an excellent mosquito repellent and disinfectant, but we had no idea about its germ-repelling properties. We simply knew it was a part of the ritual for our gods. With the fragrance of the incense and the kerosene lamps flickering, winter was the right time to tell stories and snuggle with Mother and Grandmother.

This particular night, I asked for a story I'd always been curious about. I guess each one of us has the curiosity of knowing how we were born. It's an eternal curiosity. Now that I had experienced the birth of a younger sibling, I had a burning question for my mother.

"Mom, how and when was I born?"

Mom smiled and took me on a trip down memory lane to the day I was born.

"You were born on the holy day of Janmashtami. You know what Janmashtami is."

I sort of nodded.

She said, "It is the birthday of Lord Krishna." Mom's face glowed with happiness and pride as she told me, "You were born on the day of Janmashtami, just like Lord Krishna! Lord Krishna was the child of his mother's eighth pregnancy, and you were also the child of my eighth pregnancy." Mother was elated by these similarities. "Lord Krishna's nickname was Gopal because he was a village cowboy tending their herd of cows," she went on. My mother tenderly touched me and said, "You are the son of my eighth pregnancy. That is why I named you Gopal. It is by the gods' grace that I got you. Always remember that."

But when I asked which year I was born, she was not sure.

"I don't know the year," she said, looking at me with

fondness. "You were born three years after your elder sister Gita."

So I asked my sister which year she was born and calculated my year of birth. It would be 1938 or 1939.

Mother continued her trip down memory lane, and the story was taking a very gloomy turn. She recalled the very stressful day of my birth.

"It was a windy, cloudy monsoon day. The dark clouds laden with moisture were waiting for heavy rain. Our village folks anticipated heavy rainfall. A typhoon might also hit and topple the make-believe hut in which you were to be born. Like any other childbirth, you were born in a tiny hut, built out of flimsy jute sticks that could tumble at any moment. Your grandmother prayed to her deities. In that situation, life and death were like a flip of a coin. But you were born, healthy and strong. The storm did not destroy the hut. Lord Krishna saved you, my son, don't forget that for a moment."

3

MY VILLAGE

From the time of my birth, I lived in the beautiful, self-sustaining village of Sagarkandi, Pabna, now in Bangladesh. It was a remote, underdeveloped village near the bank of the Padma river. My friends and I had never seen mountains; the lush, green fields of rice stretching endlessly to the horizon were all we knew. The vast greenness was only interrupted by small patches of dark trees.

In the fertile soil of the river valley, our crops grew almost effortlessly. In summer, the weather was humid, and the prolonged monsoon quenched the thirst of the rice, jute, garbanzo, split pea, mustard, and sugarcane plants we grew. The rising water levels during the monsoon deposited rich silt from the river, so we had very fertile land. It rained most of the year, and then came a short winter. The land was a wetland, and everything was moist, even in summer. Because of this moist climate, we knew that anything we threw on the land was going to grow.

The only thing that rose above the flat plains was the

District Board Road, a dirt road that ran from the City of Pabna to Sujanagar. Once a week, a steam-engine-driven bus would carry prisoners from the city of Pabna to the district jail in Sujanagar. The curious village kids would gather to witness this amazing machine. Besides this automobile, once in a while, a cow-drawn cart would roll by with female passengers. The vehicles left their wheel marks on the road.

Our tiny village was clustered around the District Board Road. Fifteen to twenty houses, with roofs of straw, thatch, or corrugated tin, had sprung up naturally on the elevated ground. Each individual land-owner had his or her own farmland divided into small rectangular plowable land with narrow isles as dividers, ensuring to hold rain water during the monsoon. The pieces of farmland were divided with aisles for walking. Surrounding the village, the sunny green fields of rice stretched to the horizon, as far as the eye could see.

When I was born, my village was under British rule. I lived in East Bengal, a political division of India. India had not yet been divided between Hindu-majority India and Muslim-majority Pakistan. Like any other village in rural Bengal, my village was a self-sustaining feudal society. The upper and lower castes lived together interdependently, providing each other with goods and services in exchange for work on the barter system.

Sagarkandi was unique in that it had a school, a middle English School, and a small village library where Sunday editions of a Bengali newspaper would be hand-delivered every Monday. It also had a small medicine dispensary that my elder brother would later take over. The dozen young men who were sent outside of the village to cities like Pabna, Dhaka, and Kolkata were an additional source of prosperity for the village.

The pond sat next to the narrow dirt road that went down through the center of our village. Our house was on the left. Our property was on a long stretch of land. We had a measurable size of land, an *outhouse*, a front yard, a back-yard, and a courtyard partially enclosed by the house.

Walking down the dirt path that stretched perpendicular to the district board road down the length of our property, we first walked past the vegetable garden. Next was the outbuilding where Kantu Bhai lived, which we called an *outhouse*. More like a summer house than like a toilet shack, this building was reserved for the men. Here, they gathered to discuss farmland business and smoke hookahs. It was there that I learned to smoke for the first time.

In our village, almost all men and boys used to smoke. It was a man thing. Everybody smoked. In our *outhouse*, the elderly used to assemble to smoke a *hookah*. A *hookah* is a smoking device that vaporizes tobacco. The top of the hookah contained charcoal, while the bowl crafted from a coconut shell at the bottom contained water to vaporize the substance being smoked. One or multiple people could then smoke the intricate *hookah* through a pipe. The men often sent me to the house to get fresh charcoal for their *hookah*. I would take the *kolke*, the upper part of the *hookah*, and run down to the kitchen. In the kitchen, I would ask my mother or Mamima to give me some char-coal. Carefully placing the charcoal on the *kolke*, I ran back to the *outhouse*, puffing on the coals now and then so that the fire continued burning. While doing so, I used to inhale a couple of breaths of tobacco. And that woke me up.

Suddenly, I felt I had to puff more. Even after I gave the hookah back to the older men, I craved more tobacco smoke. But the *outhouse* was out-of-bounds for children. It was reserved for the discussions of mature men, and we children were not supposed to overhear their discussions.

Pretty soon I started feeling that I needed a tobacco fix. I asked Kantu Bhai why I was having this weird desire. In reply, he advised, "Don't smoke that tobacco again. You are not supposed to smoke now. You are a child. If your mother finds out, she will kill you."

To turn his attention away from his harsh advice, I asked him, "How do you make that tobacco? It smells so good."

He felt proud. He gave me a very detailed description of how he made this tobacco. He told me, "Look behind you. Look at those tobacco plants in the back of the garden. Watch how the tobacco leaves grow." Then he added, "The leaves look like pumpkin leaves."

One time I had sneaked into the garden and tasted the tobacco leaves. Believe me, they were as bitter as hell. I told Kantu Bhai, "You wouldn't believe how bitter those leaves are."

Kantu Bhai continued with his story. He said, "When the leaves mature, we pick them up. Then we dry them in the sun in the yard."

"Yes, I know that."

"We take some dry leaves and chop them finely with the

machete. After it is properly chopped, I add some syrupy molasses and knead it well like chapati (flatbread) dough."

I understood how the tobacco was made, but it didn't satisfy my need for a tobacco fix. I decided I must look for an alternative. And I found one. Besides the elderly, most others smoked bidis, local substitutes for cigarettes. They did not have the luxury of using a hookah. The bidi was a small but very potent type of cigarette. Making them was a cottage industry and they were sold in our village market. Mama and Kantu Bhai both smoked bidis. So did lots of villagers. Bidis were a cheap alternative to cigarettes.

Once I realized that bidis would cause the same effect as the hookah, I began collecting the charred ends of the bidis that Mama would throw away after his last puff. I would collect those, keep them hidden in my pocket, and later light them, hiding them from my relatives' sight.

When walking down the dirt path perpendicular to the District Board Road, my uncle's house came right after the *outhouse*. Jyoti Mama and Mamima lived in this one-room house, which we called the Old House. Like most of the houses in the village, the Old House was made of mud. But when my father later built another standalone house, he built it with corrugated tin walls and a tin roof.

This upgraded house was called the New House, which was shaped like an L. The first side of the L was one big room, separated by three steel wardrobes which we called the almirah. On one side of the shelving was my sleeping quarters, including the big bed that my uncle had gotten as a dowry at his marriage. He had lived in that room when he moved out, so we inherited the bed. Its mattress was locally-made, but it was a real mattress, stuffed with dried coconut husks. On top were a couple of pillows. Most of the time, I slept in the bed with my mother, and my older sister and grandma would sleep on the floor on lighter mats. They slept beside our big bed or inside my grandma's little worship room.

In our sleeping area, we felt safe and comfortable. Beyond the steel wardrobes, my grandmother stored the images of her deities on a little raised pedestal. She and my parents used to worship whenever they wanted to. Past that was a little corner where a large iron safe guarded my family's money, silver, important documents, and jewelry.

Perpendicular to this long room was a smaller room, which formed the side of our L-shaped house. After my elder brother got married, he and my sister-in-law lived there for a few months. After the narrow room was a vegetarian kitchen for my grandma, where my grandma prepared her vegetarian food. It was an Indian custom that married people in our clan could eat fish and eggs. But widows had to quit these habits and become completely vegetarian. This was the expectation of the family and of the entire village. So my grandmother had a separate kitchen dedicated to her vegetarian meals. No meat or chicken was permitted in her kitchen.

Our non-vegetarian kitchen was completely separate from the vegetarian kitchen, but it was nearby, parallel to the main bedroom, forming a three-sided shape that enclosed a small yard.

Beyond the kitchens was a deep water well built with

burnt clay rings. Then came the open corrugated tin shed to store firewood and hay. Firewood was the only source of heat for cooking. No coal was available in our village or villages nearby. In the shed, Kantu Bhai also stored his eating utensils, plate, and drinking glass. Because he was Muslim, he couldn't eat on the kitchen floor or on the veranda like the rest of us. Instead, he ate in the yard, and he stored his utensils in the shed. I also noticed that his utensils were made out of enamel, not brass like ours. For most of my childhood, this seemed like an inexplicable mystery.

Next was the rice processing shed, a dedicated shed where rice was whisked into rice products. The shed housed a *dhenki ghar*, an indigenous piece of equipment that was indispensable for village life. When one *dhenki* wore out, a village carpenter named Gopal Mistry would be called in to make a new *dhenki*.

Past the *dhenki ghar*, there was a stretch of open land. At the far end of our property was our toilet shack, a few minutes' run from our bedroom. The toilet shack was a tiny tin shed perched on four bamboo poles. It had a hole in the floor where we relieved ourselves. A giant tamarind tree grew behind the shed.

All in all, we were very comfortable in our village life. My grandma loved to tell the story of how our family ended up in Sagarkandi.

"Your grandfather's father, Raghunath Podder, first settled in Sagarkandi. Your grandfather had two sons, Brojendra Kumar and Sachindra Kumar, and two daughters, Prafulla and Brojobala. The elder son, Brojendra Kumar, married your mother, who gave birth to you and your siblings."

"Do you know where your father-in-law, Raghunath, is originally from?" I asked my grandmother.

"I don't know. I only know that Raghunath, before his death, distributed his property amongst his four sons. One of whom was your grandfather." Then she told me a surprising story about how the money was distributed. "Your grandfather's father used a heavy-duty weighing scale to distribute the money."

"Why?"

"There were no paper notes then, only silver coins of one rupee denomination. Who could hand-count a giant iron safe full of coins? So he had to improvise."

"How long did it take, Grandma?"

"He did it in one day, I suppose," said Grandma.

I was amazed.

Several Podder family descendants, who were our close relatives, lived right beside us. On the right side of the dirt road, there were four more Podder families. These Podder families were the catalyst of the village. They were mostly landowners and small business owners.

To sustain the village there were families of carpenters, goldsmiths, barbers, blacksmiths, washermen, fishermen, and even some weavers. They were in close proximity to the Podders. On the outskirts of the village lived other essential folks like farmhands, peasants, caretakers, and potters.

The village also contained a Zamindar Bari, the modest mansion of the landowners in the ancient feudal system. In the entire village, only the zamindar family had a brick-and-mortar house. They also had the only boundary walls, made of six-foot high corrugated tin. The zamindars took care of the school and provided the lower-class businesspeople with goods in exchange for services. For now, our village was self-sustaining, unified, and idyllic.

But my uneducated grandfather saw the handwriting on the wall. He knew the barter system could not last forever. He began to push his children and grandchildren to get an education.

"You will need to leave the village," he said. "You will need to get educated."

One night, as the day for me to start the school approached, my mother and grandmother gathered me close for yet another story. They wanted to re-emphasize the importance of education.

"Your father married me when I was nine years old," my mother began. "This is how the story goes. Your father was a brilliant student, even in grade school. He was always first in his class. Your grandfather began to realize that things in our village were unsustainable. Even though he was very conservative and never set foot beyond that little village, he realized that things were getting unsustainable. So he pushed his two kids to get educated. Your father came to Kolkata, where a known relative was doing business as an agent of jute and rice in Bengal. Your father ended up there, studying for his matriculation. He did very well in matriculation and started going to intermediate college.

"During that time, because of our very small community of Bengalis in our caste, he lived near my elder brother who was a renowned businessman in Kolkata. They proposed to your father's father, 'We have a daughter. Get your son married, and in exchange, we will provide for his education as long as he wants to study.'

"This request was hard to turn down. Instead of a dowry, the bottom-line negotiation was that your grandfather—my father—would pay for your father's education. He could get educated as long as he wanted to.

"My brother and family said, 'OK, we will do that, but there are a couple of other conditions. You have to go and get your higher education. And until our daughter reaches fourteen, she is going to stay with us.' It is a social thing, that girls should not cohabit until after puberty. Both families agreed and we got married.

"After that, your father completed his bachelor's degree and his master's in English literature, got his law degree, and became a lawyer for Kolkata High Court. Because your grandfather initiated it, your uncle became a doctor." Later, my elder brother would become a doctor and my other brother would become a famous man in India, all because of my grandfather's initiative. He became renowned and pursued his doctorate, came to America, got his Ph.D., went back, and became a senator for India.

"Your grandfather was a completely uneducated man," my mother continued, "but he saw the handwriting on the wall. He knew we could not sustain this village way of life forever. That is why education is so important."

At that moment, with the smoke of the incense and the sweetness of my mother's arm around me, I knew deep in my heart that it was true.

4

THE JOY OF EDUCATION

Close to the time I started school, my older sister, Gita, left for Kolkata to continue her education. Three years my elder, Gita was my protector, and I was her servant. I often helped her with whatever she needed, but if I didn't feel like it, a harmless little fistfight ensued.

Gita was thin, agile, and athletic. She could leap into any tree and climb it like a monkey. Sometimes, Grandmother would ask her to bring some flowers from one of the tall trees. I'd go with her. She'd jump into the tree, scamper up its trunk, pick some flowers, and bring them to Grandma. Grandma would warn, "Gita, you have to stop climbing the trees. Pretty soon, you will no longer wear a blouse outfit. You will soon be old enough to wear a sari. If you don't do that, you are not going to get married."

But my brothers did not want their sister to be trapped in the straitjacket of village custom. In the village, no woman was allowed to study past sixth grade, which was the highest level of education offered in our village. Rather than going to Kolkata to continue their education, girls had to stay in the village and get married.

In my family, because my father was very educated, my brothers also pursued higher education. My elder brother Borda, who was a brilliant student, was studying to become a doctor in Kolkata. My next oldest brother, Chorda, had already finished sixth grade. He was continuing his education in another city where our relatives had a business. He was staying there with male family members so he could continue his 7th-10th grade education. Though I didn't know my brothers very well, I knew they cared about me and about our sister.

When Borda would come back to the village for summer vacation, he would beg my sister, "Get out of this village. If you stay here, they will force you to get married to a guy fifteen years older than you are. You will get married too early. Why don't you go help our father in Kolkata? Convince him to take you over there."

Gita listened to Borda's advice. She escaped while she still could and went to live with our father in Kolkata. She was the first woman from my village to get educated. Because she went to Kolkata at that time, she went on to later get a graduate degree. She was the first woman to get educated, just like our father was.

Finally, the day came for me to begin my own education. The school was on the opposite side of the dirt road, across from the house of Gadahar Bhuimali. The Gadahar Bhuimali family belonged to a lower caste, and they raised goats and hens.

When I was about six years old, Mama and Kantu Bhai

walked me to the only school we had in the village, Sagarkandi Middle English School, and got me admitted. According to my Jyoti Mama, my maternal uncle, this is how it happened. The headmaster was in charge of admission. He knew our family and my father very well. He asked me, "What is your birthday?"

"I don't know."

He smiled because he knew that there was no formal birth registrar office in any of the villages. So there would be no birth certificate. Jyoti Mama approximated my year of birth as 1939 and said, "Maybe you can put today's date. What date is today?"

"The eighth of November," said the headmaster, looking at a worn-out English calendar hanging from the thatched wall of his office room.

Mama nodded in agreement.

Later on in my life, when I got my school final certificate, I found out the date of my birth was recorded as November 8, 1939. And that's the way it is now. I have two birthdays: one on the holiday, Janmashtami, when my mother said I was born, and the other on the eighth of November. Lucky for me. Here in America, my friends and family celebrate both of my birthdays and pretend that they are so surprised. The other funny part is way more hilarious. Even though my wife was born on the second of October, her certificate of birth says she was born on the November 8, 1942. What a coincidence!

After I was registered, I joined the other students for the first routine of the school day. We stood in a few straight lines. The teacher came and made us recite the multiplication tables.

"Ten times two is twenty, ten times three is thirty, ten times four is forty…"

We recited all the numbers up to ten times ten. During the first couple of years of school, we would memorize multiplication tables up to twenty times twenty. For six months of the year, we would repeat this same ritual until these numbers were firmly embedded in our hypothalamuses.

The rest of the day was not as ritualistic and rote. The teacher would explain the lesson, then ask a particular student a question about the content. If he couldn't answer it, the teacher would say, "Can anyone else answer the question?"

If another student piped up, "Yes, I can answer the question," then that student was allowed to twist the first child's ear. It was very embarrassing to be on the receiving end of this humiliation, so I immediately made a goal: "Whenever they ask me a question, I'm going to get it right."

But this wasn't the end of the humiliation. Each teacher carried a cane in his hand. If a student failed to answer a question, besides the humiliation of having his ear twisted, he would receive corporal punishment. The teacher would ask the child to open his palm, and the teacher would hit him with the cane. He didn't hit him too severely, but the student would have a red mark on his palm for a while.

The school building was a long, L-shaped school. There were four classrooms in the school along the long side of the L. Each room was about ten feet by twelve feet, and they housed Class 1-2 (grades 1-2), Class 3 in its own room, Class 4 by itself, and Classes 5-6 combined. On the small side of the L were two small rooms: an admin office for the headmaster, who was both the administrator and overseer of the school, and a room for teachers.

In school, we learned math, history, geography, English, and Bengali. We started school around nine or ten in the morning when we heard the sound of the bell. Since there were no packaged lunches, lunchboxes, or grocery stores in those days, we had to come home to eat. We had our lunch at around two o'clock in the afternoon when we were done with school for the day.

Historically, education in India was propagated by the Brahmin, the highest caste. I learned about the Brahmin one day when I saw my mother and grandmother bowing down to the Brahmin village priests. In our village, the custom was that you should bow to anybody older than you. You should touch your knee to the ground and bow down your head to the ground to pay homage. That was the standard: if anyone older than you walked up to your house, you would respect them with one of the two types of bows: namaste or pranam.

The priests were Brahmin. There were two priests in our village, and they would come once a week. The whole family would stand outside and perform a ritual bow. When I saw my mother and grandmother bowing to the village priests, I was confused.

"Why did you bow to these guys, even though they are not older?"

"Even though they are not older, they are Brahmin."

"Why?"

"That is the standard culture of the caste system."

I eventually learned that the bottom caste contained untouchables, people like servants, maids, and cremation attendants. The next caste, which we belonged to, was the business class, or Vaishya. We made our living by doing business. The next caste was the warrior class, and next came a caste of literate people who were the authorized agents of god. Though there were other villagers who were literate, the education system was stewarded by the Brahmin. If you wanted to get educated, the Brahmin would help you get educated. They had little places where students could go and learn, and small verandas for getting educated.

I knew there was a difference between us and the Brahmin. I also knew there was a difference between us and the Muslims, who belonged to a lower class. But all in all, we coexisted peacefully. I recall a specific incident that illustrates how well Muslims and Hindus got along in those days. Our Bengali teacher taught us about the unity of Hindus and Muslims.

"Hindus and Muslims are two leaves of the same stem," the teacher said. "When Islamic conquerors first entered our nation in 1021 AD, the people of India realized that the Mughals were better than most conquerors. Even though the Mughals were not saints, we realized they had not come to exploit us and send our goods elsewhere. Instead, they came to stay. They enlisted Hindus as part of their feudal kingdoms. All over India, Muslims and Hindus began to work for the emperor. The Mughal Empire was a very wealthy and peaceful nation. They lived in harmony, but that doesn't mean there was no exploitation. It was more like the exploitation of kings and their subjects, rather than the exploitation of a foreign entity that sent everything back to the mother-country.

"The Hindus and Muslims in our nation cooperated, even reading each other's scriptures and adopting each other's religious practices. Some Islamic leaders believed the Hindu scriptures were inspired by the gods. They rubbed themselves with ashes or hung upside down while praying, like the Hindus. The two religions almost merged into one. Hindus believed the Muslim Sultan was the god Vishnu in human form. Muslims presented offerings at the Hindu places of worship and Hindus visited the graves of important Muslim leaders. A Muslim priest translated an important Hindu document into his language. He wrote a book called *The Mingling of Two Oceans* to emphasize the ways the two religions are alike. So you can see that Muslims and Hindus are closely related. They have lived together in harmony for many years."

As I listened, I knew it was true. I rarely saw any animosity between the classes. The Muslims were tolerated and allowed to coexist. The middle classes carried on with their business ventures, and the highly respected Brahmin Hindus were entrusted with education.

Education changed when the British came in 1858. They started primary schools or middle English schools in villages. The kids would go to school in the village up to sixth grade, and then most village children would stay in the village doing whatever they chose to do for a living. Very few of them went to Kolkata or other cities to get higher education.

But from the beginning of my life, I was always forced to study, with the understanding that I would go away from the village to finish school, just like my brothers did. There was one requirement in my family: that I must study and finish school. The headteacher lived only a block away from us, and if I slacked off on any of my subjects, he would come and report to my mother. "Your kid is not doing very well," he would say. It was the local way of taking care of every kid.

We went to school eleven months out of the year. Even during summer, we studied every morning and into the early afternoon. After school on long summer evenings, my friends and I were always outside. There was no supervision; we were left to our own devices.

During those long hours of roaming free in the village after school, every adult in the village helped with the responsibility of disciplining us children. One day, my relative and neighbor Gnan Da brought an amazing new apparatus into the village.

"A relative from Kolkata brought something that sings," said Panu, my friend and closest ally in doing mischief. "It is called a gramophone."

Full of curiosity, I began begging Gnan Da, "Let me see it! How does it work?"

The whole village, eight to ten families, gathered in Gnan Da's house and listened to the new machine. We watched in awe as Gnan Da cranked the machine and music began crackling out of the huge golden bell.

"How does the man who sings hide in such a small space?" I wondered.

After the spectacle was over, I determined to find out. I pulled aside one of the girls in the family, who was the same age as Panu and me.

"Please," I said, "make an agreement with me. Let me and Panu come in and investigate the contraption. We need to find out where the sound is coming from."

So the girl let us into the house. As the gramophone played, we searched all around the house. But we couldn't find anything. My curiosity was getting the best of me.

"Where is that guy hiding?"

Finally, I went to the girl's father, Gnan Da, and asked him, "You know that machine that you played? Where is the sound coming from? There is no one hiding there, so where is the voice coming from?"

"What?" Gnan was curious.

"I went to your house in the afternoon and looked at it."

Gnan Da's face turned dark with anger. He slapped me so hard I fell to the ground. When I got up, I slunk quietly home. I knew that if I complained to my mother, I would only get beaten a second time. The whole village was a part of the grand scheme of discipline.

The village not only disciplined me for my curiosity, but also for my misdeeds. One time while I was trying to smoke a bidi in secret, I got caught by a stranger. With a strong rebuke, he slapped me for my misdeed. Any time someone saw us doing something wrong, they would push or shove us and say, "Don't do that." There was no recourse when a village member disciplined us. If I complained to my mother, she would just say, "You deserved it."

Even though there was no direct adult supervision and we did not have adults to entertain us and shuttle us around to various activities, we did not get bored. Our minds and imaginations were rich, so we had no shortage of things to do. The village was so poor that we didn't have standard soccer balls, but that was no problem for us. We used green grapefruit instead. These hard, green, lightly pimpled spheres worked perfectly for balls. In our small village, there were always four or five of us goofing around and doing things we could think of to entertain ourselves.

5

STORIES AFTER DARK

One of our most frequent modes of entertainment was going to the pond. At the center of my village was a large, man-made pond. This pond was dug a long time ago by the Zamindars, the ancient ruling families of the village. These long-ago excavators piled the dirt all around the sides of the pond, so the bank of the pond was still elevated.

The pond was surrounded by concrete terraces that doubled as benches. These terraces reached part of the way around the pond's perimeter. On three sides of the pond, the terraces formed U-shaped indentations, each containing a set of stairs leading down through the middle of the terraces. People walked down the cement steps into the water. These flights of stairs were called *ghats*.

One *ghat* was in front of the pond, facing the District Board Road. The front of the pond doubled as the village square, and older men used to gather there to gossip about what was going on in the village. Two other *ghats* were located on the left and right sides of the pond. Men and boys used the front *ghat* for bathing, while the other two *ghats* were designated for women and girls coming from the other two sides of the village. All four banks of the pond were pitted with a variety of unknown tropical trees, shrubs, and weeds. A tamarind tree stood tall beside the pond, and a grove of mangoes stretched along the back of the pond.

The hot summer days were nearly unbearable because of the very high humidity. Most houses were very hot because of their tin roofs. So after school, we kids headed for the pond. We couldn't wait to grab some mango and tamarind and sit under the shade of a tree. So as soon as we got home from school, we put some salt and chili pepper in our little matchboxes and set off for the pond.

In the grove behind the pond, we gathered green mangoes in our *gamchas*. *Gamchas* were long pieces of cloth, two feet by three feet, that we usually wore tied around our waists. They had so many uses. After a dip in the pond, we could use them as a towel. When it was too hot, we could swipe the sweat off our faces like a kerchief. And when we needed to carry something, we could use them as a bag. We'd roll these mangoes into the *gamchas* and carry them to the edge of the pool. We broke them against the concrete, ripped them open, and put in salt and chili pepper from our matchboxes. Then we ate them with relish.

Mangoes were a main staple fruit in our village, the most important fruit in our society. Every house had at least one mango tree. The Himsagar mangoes that grew in our part of Bengal were very fragrant and sweet. From the time they started surrounding our homes with aromatic white blossoms in January, we began excitedly waiting for them to be ready. We ate mangoes green and ripe. Mangoes were so abundant that we made pulp and dried it to make a treat similar to fruit loops. Our village had more than ten types of mangoes, ranging from sour to super sweet and everywhere in between. They were Bengal's most cherished fruit, almost a national fruit of Bengal.

After we ate our mangoes, we often jumped into the pond to cool down. Then we would climb the tamarind tree and eat the tart green tamarinds. They were so sour they made our cheeks pucker. The giant tamarind tree spread its tangled branches and twigs above our heads, creating a massive area of cool, refreshing shade. When I looked at it, I felt that the tree was like a tall Indian sadhu medicine man, standing still in a trance with a giant mass of tangled hair.

But even as I felt awed by the mystical look of the tree, I began to feel fearful. I tried not to think about the story my grandmother had told me after dark… about the ghosts, witches, and mythical spirits that attached themselves to big trees like this one. But I couldn't keep it out of my mind.

"Don't go near the tamarind tree," she would begin. "The ghosts and the witches hiding there will come out and eat you alive." I listened with a mixture of fear and excitement as she launched into the story. "The shaak-chunni is the ghost of an unpurified living thing," she said. "She is a tree-spirit that latches onto trees. She is extremely ugly and hideous but can shape-shift and disguise herself as a beautiful woman to lure men into the woods or mountains. Then she kills them and sucks up their life. She eats them alive! Women who die during childbirth will come back in revenge as a shaak-chunni.[1] The woman whose birth shack burned may come back to haunt the people who did not save her. She may be in that tree right now. Don't go near it."

I now know that Grandma intentionally scared me so I would not go there alone and get lost. In a village without direct supervision, scare tactics were the best tool for keeping children safe. Ghost stories and stories of strangers kidnapping children were her way to ensure safety for me! But as I look back, I believe these stories did more harm than good.

As I stood in front of the tamarind tree, I tried to chase the story out of my mind. The sun was setting, and I knew my mother would soon want me home. Year round, the whole village woke up with the sun and wound down when the sun set. I knew my mother would have supper ready for me, and that soon she would yell at me to start studying.

"You goofed around with your friends all evening!" she'd say, just like every day. "Now do something or you will get punished."

So I headed home down the little dirt path, past the vegetable garden, the *outhouse*, the front yard, the old and the new houses, straight into the kitchen where supper was waiting for me. We typically ate four meals: breakfast in the morning, lunch in the early afternoon, pressed rice with milk and sugar in the afternoon, and dinner after the sun went down, whenever Mother and Grandmother had it ready. My favorite food was rice. I loved cooked rice, and I also loved rice that had been boiled to make a sweet rice puree called "fanna bhat." Once in a while, we would have it in the morning for breakfast with a little bit of mashed potato and ghee, which is clarified butter. For supper, we ate rice with ghee and hot pepper, lentil or split pea dhal, cooked vegetables, fish, and sweet rice dessert.

After dark on school days, we ate our four-course dinner and then started our evenings by studying. We had a little study spot near our bed. Our kerosene lamps and one lantern were the only things we had to light the darkness. We carried that lamp from place to place, wherever we needed light. At night, we completed our school assignments, studied, and read books in front of the lamps.

One of the most important books I read was the ballad of Ramayana. It was about three hundred pages long, a lovely poem with 24,000 verses.[2] It was the story of the love and dedication of Rama, who was exiled to the forest with his Beloved, Sita. A ten-headed evil antagonist, a twenty-armed beast named Ravana, kidnapped Sita. Rama had to be creative in rescuing her. Thankfully, Sita had left a trail of jewelry to help Rama find her. As he followed the trail, Rama found a monkey king, Hanuman. He sent messages to "all the monkeys in the world, who set out to find Sita."[3]

Finally, Rama found his beloved Sita on the island of Lanka, held captive by Ravana. Nala, a monkey who was the son of an architect-god, decided to help Rama build a bridge across the water to the island. The monkeys cut down mighty trees, cut the logs, and placed them on top of giant boulders they had thrown into the sea. Together, the monkeys completed an eighty-mile bridge in just five days. The bridge, called Rama Setu, was complete. The army of animals, which included monkeys, bears, and other creatures, passed over the bridge and fought the evil king Ravana. Rama shot a magic arrow and killed Ravana. Because of their courage, Sita was finally safe.

I loved this ballad: its poetry, its artistry, and the dramas that were based on this poem. My love for artistic things started very early, and I noticed the beauty of the rhythmic meter of accented and unaccented syllables in this poem. The ballad used art and poetry to communicate the triumph of good over evil and the importance of sacrificial commitment to those you loved.[4]

The Ramayana touched me deeply. I read these tales with childhood awe and fascination. There seemed to be a god for every type of ailment imaginable. There were no doctors nearby, so when I had a belly ache, I invented a god in my mind. I murmured his name, and the bellyache would go away. My faith continued to grow. As I watched my grandmother and mother worshiping their gods, I started feeling that there would be a supernatural power that would help me, no matter what.

By the time I was eight or nine years old, I had memorized almost every page in the Ramayana. I read every line. I knew everything by heart. These stories were so fascinating and important to me. They spoke to the artistic side of me, the side that adored drama. Studying the Ramayana barely felt like schoolwork.

After we finished our studies, my grandmother would begin telling stories. We snuggled in close to see what she would tell us today.

"Once upon a time there was a king. The king had two wives," she began. "He married the second wife because the first wife didn't have any kids. After he married the second wife, she also didn't have any kids, so they went to a priest and asked, 'What can you do to give us a child?' The priest said, 'Take these herbs, go home, make a paste, and have your wife the queen drink it.' So they came home and ground the herbs with a mortar and pestle. The main queen ground the herbs, made a paste, and ate it. When the other queen saw it, she said to herself, 'After the first queen disappears, I will also go eat some of it.' In the meantime, a snake crawled over the grinding stone. Because the younger queen licked the herbs, which had been contaminated by the snake, she eventually gave birth to two snakes. The older queen had a little daughter. One day, after they had grown up a little bit, the little girl realized she had two brothers who both were snakes. She began to go to a nearby pond and wait for them to appear. One day, they appeared. They took her on their back and swam to a small island, where they lived. This went on for some time. Finally one day, these two snake brothers gave their sister a precious jewel. On a regular basis, the sister would take some milk to that place and these two snakes would come and drink it. One day, the second queen saw what was going on. She poisoned the milk and the two snake brothers died. The end."

"Grandma, what happened after that?"

"We don't know, we don't know."

After we ate and the storytelling was over, we went to bed. There was no clock, but we knew it was time to fall asleep so we could be ready for school tomorrow. As we fell asleep, the only sound was the gentle wind in the trees.

At midnight, we heard a loud thud. It came from the

palm trees across the little road that ran perpendicular to the pond. On the other side of our neighbors' property, a palm fruit fell from the tree and hit the ground with a thud. Instantly jumping out of bed, we grabbed our lanterns and ran to see if we could be the first to claim the palm fruit. Large like a pumpkin, these palm fruits tasted tart and delicious.

After snacking on the palm fruit, we hurried back to bed to get some sleep before another day of school. We knew that seasons were changing, and before long, we'd be going to sleep to the sound of steady rain. The monsoon season was coming.

6

CHANGING SEASONS

"I'm here to check your boat and dinghies." Gopal Mistry and his siblings stood at our door one day. "Do you have any leaks? Do you need a repair or a fresh coat of water-repellant bitumen coating?"

We had no calendar, but whenever we saw Gopal Mistry and his siblings going from house to house to check everyone's boats and dinghies, we knew it was time for another rainy season.

Soon the monsoon began. Rain began to fall most of the day, turning the fields to mud. When the rain paused temporarily, I looked out over the fields below our village and watched the villagers planting rice. They stooped in their rice fields, methodically placing clumps of rice sprouts in the moist mud.

The rice grew. When it was not raining, the flooded fields glowed a gorgeous green in the evening sunshine. The rice plants danced in the wind, and insects and frogs sang softly and rhythmically in the fields.

Heavy rain came every day. The water began to rise, taking over the shallow rice paddies first, then rising to the elevation of the village and creeping over our land. But miraculously, the growing rice and jute were never underwater. They continued to grow in rhythm with the rise of the water level. Jute plants, whose leafy tops and long slender stems were mostly underwater, would be harvested later in the year, and the fibers from their stems would be used to create rope. The natural fiber was strong, insulating, and breathable. It was used for insulation, wall coverings, flooring, garments, rugs, ropes, gunny sacks, curtains, paper, sandals, bags, and furniture.[1] Jute was in demand around the world, and the barter of jute helped sustain our village's economy. But for now, the jute was a leafy green field flooded with monsoon water. As the water rose, so did the heads of the jute trees. They grew like crazy: acres and acres and acres of cultivated land.

The dense, leafy jute fields were perfect places to hide. After I got addicted to smoking, I had to find ways to smoke without my parents catching me. In India in those days, if we were caught smoking bidis, we would be punished severely by anybody who saw us. We would be given two slaps by anyone who walked by and happened to see us smoking. The jute field was a perfect place to smoke undetected.

The water had already risen to the level of the District Board Road, so my friends and I hopped into a dinghy and paddled out to the jute fields. There, in seclusion, we could puff away on our bidi and then paddle back home. Our parents never saw us.

During the monsoon season, the rain joined with the frogs, insects, and the wind to create a beautiful symphony of nature. Gentle winds, rougher gales, ragged storms, and full-blown cyclones were the bass notes. Rain pinging on the tin roof formed the high staccato. In the background, the rice kept growing and growing, waving in the wind in an unbelievable synergy, dancing to the music of nature.

All the while, we were safe inside our snug home. Above and around us, water droplets fell steadily, watering the mango trees that soaked up the moisture like a thirsty chital deer drinking at a stream. The smell of rain was incredibly comforting and familiar, part of the poetry of the season. An indescribable scent filled our nostrils: the aroma of tropical plants, deep humidity, and the raw, dark soil. It was a natural smell, beautiful beyond words.

Storms and flooding were normal life to us. The water levels continued to rise, all the way up to the floors of our homes. Even though the homes were on a raised area, they were still on generally flat land. To compensate, all houses were built on stilts at least three feet high. When the water rose very high, we couldn't walk from our bedroom to our kitchen. We had to use a dinghy. As kids, we picked up the necessary skills very quickly. We climbed in our little boat, stuck a bamboo pole in the ground, applied a little pressure, and propelled our dinghy toward our kitchen. We rowed to the kitchen, and we rowed to school. We also learned to swim before we were four or five years old.

The monsoon season lasted from mid-June to the end of August or the middle of September. The rice would mature after the monsoon, in October or November. The rain would slowly diminish, the water would subside, and the tall rice stalks would droop with their long, pale golden heads of rice.

Then the harvest began. Workers crouched low in the fields, slicing the rustling bundles of rice. Insects sang. They carried the bundles to our yard and loosened the twine, letting the stalks and heads of rice fall onto a large piece of burlap. We tied up two beautiful fawn-colored cows and made them walk in a circle to thresh the rice. The cows did not pull a threshing implement; they simply trampled the pile of loose rice until the grains of rice fell out. Two guys led the cows while the third gathered the stalks of rice that fell off the pile and used a long stick to shove them back into the middle again. After pushing the dry rice grass away and shaking it to make sure no rice stayed in the head, we had a pile of grain.

Our mother and grandmother poured huge bowls of rice grains into a vat of water and soaked them. Then they stuffed rice straw into the fire under the vat and parboiled it. Finally, they dried the grains of rice in the sun during the early and late winter. After it was dry, they pounded the rice until the husks fell off.

They de-husked it with the dhenki, a long wooden beam that sat like a seesaw over a fulcrum. One end of the beam had a vertical wooden pestle. When a woman repetitively raised and lowered one end of the horizontal beam, the vertical pestle went up and down and pounded the raw paddy rice, which was in a hole in the floor.

At least two women would operate the dhenki. One would peddle the flat end of the horizontal wooden beam, causing the ramrod to move rhythmically up and down. The other woman sat near the hole in the ground, carefully and skillfully sweeping the rice back into the indentation and moving the husks away. She worked to the rhythm of the moving anvil, aware that the falling ramrod could crush her hand if misplaced. When the women finished, they had a pile of beautiful, translucent rice grains. Since they were parboiled, they could be prepared with very little cooking.

After the husks were pounded off the rice grains, the rice could also be ground to flour using the same contraption. The women could pound the rice until it was a smooth, white powder. Or they could press the parboiled rice into thin, translucent rice flakes, which were like cereal and could be eaten as a delicious morning snack, with or without milk.

After the rice harvest came a time of year that we looked forward to year-round: Durga Puja. This religious holiday was the only time we had a month-long break from school. On the lunar calendar, Durga Puja starts at the end of September or the first week of October. For an entire month, we were free to enjoy Puja and its rituals from dawn to dusk. The entire village was busy enjoying it. It was a festive month.

Without a calendar, how did we know when Durga Puja was about to happen? When the waters of the monsoon started receding, large boats would arrive via the Padma and dock alongside the District Board Road with loads of coconut, sugar, and other supplies for making homemade treats. We'd go to the riverbank and see heaps of coconuts, enough for the entire village. A representative of each village household would heave several coconuts to his shoulders and carry them back to the house. How our parents could afford to buy these luxuries, we had no idea. We could hardly wait for the homemade sweets that we knew our mother would make!

My caregivers, Jyoti Mama, and Kantu Bhai broke open the coconuts. Inside was coconut water, a delicious treat. Kantu Bhai would save the coconut water and set it aside, and we would drink it. After de-husking the bright white meat, they gave it to my mother, grandmother, and auntie inside the house. The women shredded the coconut meat with a serrated tool, scraping off the white curls of coconut. After it was serrated, they cooked the coconut meat in milk with sugar or molasses. Then they shaped it into little balls called Naru. While they cooked, we waited outside the kitchen. We sat nearby, begging, "Please give me one or two."

They made the same type of treat out of rice or sesame seeds. To make this homemade dessert, they would grind the rice and soak it in water. Then they made very tiny balls and dried them. Then they added molasses and cooked them to make little rice Naru.

In addition to boatloads of sweets, artists from another village began to arrive to build an image of the idols of Durga Pratima. Chaitanya Pal was an artisan who would arrive with two or three other artisans a few months before the holiday to build the Durga Pratima image. Chaitanya was more than an artisan. He was a sculptor and an idol maker of the goddess Durga. Every year, he and his helpers would recreate a new scene that contained four to five images of the gods.

The goddess Durga was always worshiped together with her two daughters and two sons. One daughter was the goddess of learning and education, and the other was the goddess of fortune and money. Durga's sons were Lord Ganesha, a demigod who was famous in India for his elephant head, and Lord Karttikeya, the god of war. The entire scene with all five gods was eight to ten feet tall and ten to twelve feet wide. I was obsessed with watching how they built the images.

"Come on, Panu, let's go see!" I said.

"Yes!" Panu agreed, following me.

When we arrived at the spot where the artisans were building, we saw Chaitanya Pal and his helpers hard at work. They sat on the ground inside the Mandop, the shed where the images would be housed during the festivities. The artisans would grab a loose bundle of straw, then deftly wrap it with jute twine along its entire length. During the process of wrapping the bundle in string, they would shape the bundle. Some of the bundles were thicker at one end than at the other. The artisans trimmed off excess straw at the end of the bundles, which were now curved into the shape of a leg, an arm, an elephant trunk, a shapely hip and knee, a torso, or some other part of the deities. The artisans made bundle after bundle and tied them onto each other. A torso, a pair of hips and knees, and ten arms came together to form Durga herself. They tied Durga onto a wooden lattice frame. Below her curved the thick straw body of the lion she was conquering.

After they tied each god or goddess onto the frame, they hacked dry clods of dirt and clay into small pieces, put it onto a large tarp, added water, and began stomping, mixing, and kneading it into a usable clay paste. They added jute cuttings or rice husks to the clay to create a binding material. One by one, they coated the straw bodies, legs, arms, and faces with the soft material.

The final touch was to apply refined clay. They smoothed it over the rough forms and meticulously shaped the details of the bodies and intricate, ornate borders of the backdrops. They used a mold for the head of each god. After the clay in the mold was dried, they mounted the head on the body. The heads had very finely crafted expressions: eyes, noses, and even teeth on the lion.

The last touch was dressing the images of the gods. They painted the statues with rich pigments and decorated them with clothes and jewelry. Panu and I watched in fascination as this process unfolded. It took days to finish the scene. But after it was complete, Panu and I looked at each other in awe.

"Let us build one for our house!" we decided.

"Maybe Chaitanya Pal will help us! He is a great man."

"Yes!"

Quickly, we gathered bundles of straw and started to tie the bundles into shapes with twine. Though the official statues were larger, our statues were about three feet wide and two to three feet tall.

Panu was more skillful than I was. But I did my best. I kneaded the wet clay with my bare hands and smeared it over the straw bundles. Chaitanya Pal himself stopped by one day to help us, give us advice, and coach us in any way he could. He was a great artist, and his help was invaluable.

We worked hard to complete all five images. When we were done, we stood back in awe and gazed at our handiwork.

"Now we need to get a priest to bless our statues and ceremonially bring them to life."

But no priest would come to worship the images. There was a series of rituals we would have to do to get ready for the priest to come and bring the gods to life. Without a priest, nothing religious could take place. They were gate-keepers, and they would not bless our statues.

Finally, our parents told us to give up on the idea of having a priest come. "Listen Gopal, listen Panu, worshiping gods is not a child's game. The priests are not going to come. It's not going to happen," they said.

So we worshiped the statues the way we thought we should perform them. The next year, when we tried to build the statues, we were told, "You cannot do that. That's not religiously permissible."

7

BALLAD OF RAMAYANA

From my earliest memories, I was fascinated by the rituals of my religion, and I loved the artistic and poetic expression of my beliefs. Another religious event that I deeply enjoyed was the ballad of the Ramayana. The ballad was going on full steam. Jaladhar Bayen, the famous local ballad, had recently arrived in our village. The news of his arrival started spreading all over the village. The preparations went on for more than a week. The helping hands designated by my paternal uncle, Jathamosai, had finished building a temporary raised platform in the Nat Mandir. The Nat Mandir was an open, expansive tin shed used for special village gatherings. The Mandir was located in between the worship room and Jathamosai's *outhouse*.

My mother and grandmother said that the Bayen would perform the stories of Ramayana for two consecutive nights. The first night, he would narrate the story of the epic war between Rama and Ravana. The second night would be the episode of how Rama traveled to meet Sita and married her.

The story came from the Ramayana, one of the most sacred ancient books that most of the villagers owned. Years ago, the poet Kirtibash had written the Bengali version of this book in rhymes. Every evening, my mother or grandmother would recite these rhymes to a traditional melody.

I was very excited. Even though most of us were very familiar with the story of Rama and Ravana, it was the performance that mattered. We were required to attend these rituals, but I would have attended of my own free will. I loved the dramatic events narrated in the book. Sometimes I even dreamed that Rama was losing to Ravana, and woke up in distress.

Jaladhar Bayen would stay with Jathamosai, my paternal uncle. My mother explained who Bayen was.

"Bayen is a traveling folk poet. He is a very respected Brahmin, a very pious man, and a celibate. He eats only one meal a day."

My jaw dropped and my eyes widened. How could a man survive eating only one meal? We were used to eating at least four times a day! Later, I gathered three or four of my friends.

"We need to figure out how this man survives on only one meal! We must find out what he eats!"

My friends agreed. So we sneaked to the house where he was staying and peeked in the door. Bayen was a tall but thin man with a protruded belly. Bayen was sitting on the kitchen floor near the fire pit of Jathamosai's kitchen. A local widow was helping him to prepare his own meal. As

Panu, my other friends and I peeped in from outside, we saw that Bayen was cooking a one-pot meal with a variety of vegetables, rice, and split pea dhal. He added a generous amount of ghee. It was a sumptuous khichudi with ghee. My mouth started watering.

After he cooked the meal, the widow brought him a banana leaf and a glass full of water. He washed his hands and sprinkled water around the banana leaf, murmuring unintelligible mantras. He then started taking the food out of the cooking pot. We couldn't believe what an enormous heap of food he stacked on the banana leaf. Even a cat couldn't jump over the heap!

It took a long time for him to finish the food. He took one gulp at a time and swallowed it with relish. Suddenly, as we watched him eat, the widow noticed us.

"Get away! Go home!" she shouted. "Do you want me to call your mother? Little devils."

We dispersed, scampering to our respective homes to wait for the night's festivities. Finally, the evening came. Tonight, he would perform the battle of Ram and Ravana. Jyoti Mama and two other caretakers were placing the hazak lamps around the platform. Since there was no electricity, we used these technologically advanced lamps for lighting. Hazak lamps emitted a very bright light, twenty times more powerful than normal kerosene lamps. They had filaments that glowed like electric lights. Although hazak lamps were powered by kerosene or paraffin like any other lamp, they were made of brass or silver and had an oil tank, a tube, and a vaporizing chamber. Hazak lamps created light through high-pressure, heated vapor that powered them for three hours, long enough to light the stage.

The stage was almost ready. My mother, my grandmother, and all our close family members were in the front row. So was the Zamindar family. The rest of the nat mandir was filled with other villagers. Anticipation built as Bayen appeared on the stage. A gasp went through my group of friends as we saw the transformation that had taken place in Bayen's appearance. He wore a long white dhoti and a knee-high panjabi. He had a tan silk waistband. His wrist displayed a colorful garland of flowers, and in his right hand he was holding a *chamar*, a fly whisk. It was rumored that they made the *chamars* from the long hairy tails of Chamar cows.

Bayen started the ballad of the battle of Rama with Ravana. The performance was centered around Bayen, who was the main performer. He had three accompanists sitting at the back. Bayen would dance, mimic a battle cry, and sing a few lines from Ramayana. Then the attendants would echo him, repeating the same lines with gusto. They would clash their cymbals, beat their drums, and play the harmonium. This was how the entire story would be performed.

As the intensity of the performance increased, so did the tempo. Bayen impersonated all the different characters in the ballad: first Rama, then Ravana, then other characters. Bayen was eclectic and unpredictable, waving the cow-tail *chamar*. As we sat in the audience, transfixed, it was as if the *chamar* was transforming into Lord Rama's bow. He would pull out the imaginary arrows from Rama's quiver. Then he transformed into Rama. He used arrows of fire, storm, and flood. I could feel it, and so could the rest of the audience. His performance was spellbinding and divine. The characters were coming to life.

Like all good things, the performance came to an end. As the last haunting note of the harmonium faded away, my amazement only grew. I imagined how I could be a ballad performer like him. I really wanted to try.

A few days passed. I was playing marbles with Panu and a few others.

"Rammangal is so mind-boggling!" Panu said. Rammangal was another name for the Ballad of Ramayana. "It was so amazing!"

"Yes," I said, "and I also noticed that my mother and grandmother were giving the Bayen some homemade sweets, some garments and a couple of silver coins."

"They bowed down and touched Bayen's feet. He must be a respectable man!"

We were silent for a moment. Then I confided in Panu, "I have an idea."

"What is it?"

"Let's form a Rammangal team."

He said, "What?"

"We can form a Rammangal team."

"You must be crazy," he said.

I said, "What's wrong with trying? Think how many sweets we could get!"

"You and I cannot form a team. We need more people."

I started to outline a plan that was forming in my mind. I said, "Look, I will be the main performer. All we need is two or three kids to join us. You are already one."

"No, not me," Panu said.

"Why not?"

"I don't know how to sing."

"You don't have to sing. You just play the cymbals."

After a lot of discussions, Panu agreed. We gathered two more kids. One was Gopal Mistry's son, and the other was Madhusudan, the son of our barber. We discovered Panu was not good at cymbals. So we assigned Panu to play the drum instead. But where could we find a drum? Nobody was going to give us one. We improvised the drum with an empty earthenware pot. Panu was an expert in tapping the side of the pot to sound like a *tabla* or a drum. We got a pair of cymbals from my grandmother. Eventually, we formed a team and started performing in our *outhouse*, without anybody's knowledge. As we practiced, we gained confidence. But who was going to host us? We were very shy about approaching anybody.

One day, something surprising happened. A widow, known as Sudheer's Ma, was taking a bath in the pond. Everybody knew her. She was very particular about making sure that she completely submerged her entire body underwater so that she would feel completely sanitized. That day, she asked me, "Gopal, please make sure that I completely submerge my head deep in the water."

I said, "Sure, I will."

"Was I able to do it?" she asked when she bobbed out of the water, her long gray hair drenched with lake water.

Panu gave me a mischievous look and shook his head. I understood Panu's naughty intention. So I said, "No."

She tried to submerge her head in the water, once, twice,

and three times. Finally, I felt pity for her and also a little guilty. I told her, "You did perfectly alright. Please don't worry."

She thanked us. I hesitantly asked her if she would be interested in Rammangal. I told her that we formed a Rammangal team so we could perform and sing.

"Why don't you perform it at my place?"

We were excited and told her, "When do you want us to perform?"

"How about this afternoon."

That was the start of our Rammangal venture. That afternoon, we performed the episode of Rama's marriage to Sita. She assembled a few other devoted widows and married women to witness our childish performance. After our ballad was finished, we could tell that our audience enjoyed the event.

"How soon can you perform again?" Sudheer's mother asked us.

We were thrilled. "We will come back soon," we promised.

As a reward, she fed us some homemade sweets and blessed us. After that day, I promised myself that I would never play tricks on her again. I never knew she was so good and generous.

The news of our kids' Rammangal group was spreading fast in our little village. One day, my mother asked, "I hear that you formed a Rammangal group? Is that right?"

I was concerned that my mother wouldn't like it. So I hesitated.

"I am surprised that you memorized the whole

Ramayana from the ballad Bayen performed. But don't neglect your studies. Reciting and singing the god's name will help you achieve anything you want," she added.

I was grateful for my mother's praise, and I knew that this was my opportunity to ask her something that had been on my mind for a long time. I had never had the courage to ask her, but I realized that this was the opportunity.

"Ma, can you ask Jyoti Mama to make a bow and some arrows for me?"

My mother looked at me with inquiring eyes.

"I want to become an expert at shooting a bow and arrow like the god Rama. I will then be able to kill any enemies who may harm us."

My mother hugged me and gently said, "How come you are having all these weird thoughts in your brain? Don't worry. I will ask Jyoti to make you the bow and arrows. Are you happy now?"

I hugged her back. The next day, Jyoti Mama began making the bows and arrows. I sat nearby, watching each and every move he made. I noticed how he held a piece of bamboo and split it with the cutlass. How his skilled hand was refining the bamboo slats and shaping them into the bow. It amazed me to see how he used the cutlass to make a round bamboo stick and transform it into an arrow. He made a few of them. Then he walked into the *outhouse* and brought a piece of jute rope. Skillfully, he tied the rope and bent the slat into a bow. Then he handed them over to me.

"Do you know how to shoot an arrow?" he asked.

I shook my head no.

"Let me show you how," Mama said.

After he demonstrated, I eagerly grabbed the bow and arrow to try it myself. But it was harder than it looked. On my first several attempts, I failed to hit the mark. I placed a little bamboo stand against a tree on our property and tried over and over to hit it. I practiced and practiced, even though I kept missing the mark. Finally, I made it. With more practice, I got good enough that I could hit the target every time. Equipped with my new bow and arrow, I went into the bamboo jungle and pretended I was killing the evil Ravana with my arrows.

"I am becoming Rama," I thought with excitement.

8

INNOCENCE LOST

Despite my fascination with my religion, I gradually began to notice other traditions that were not as beautiful. Throughout my childhood, I had seen our religious customs with rose-colored glasses. At first, the customs seemed normal, even beautiful. But as I grew, my perspective on life began changing. I could see both the good and the bad, and I started judging our rituals. I started thinking about child marriage, the way untouchables were treated, and other superstitious rites in our village. I pondered the tragic death of the mother and newborn baby in the birth hut. As I grew older, I gradually began to see how wrong these rituals were.

One incident in particular changed my attitude toward my religious belief forever. At school, we found out there was going to be a Kabaddi competition. Kabaddi is a game that was very popular in our village, as it was in the entire area. Today, Kabaddi is the national sport of Bangladesh, which is the name given to the area surrounding Sagarkandi today.

Kabaddi is like a competitive game of tag. We would form two teams, ideally made of seven players each, on a wide, flat piece of land. The playing field was divided into two sections. The teams took turns going on the offensive. A person from one team ventured into the other team's area to tag as many people as possible without getting knocked over and tackled. If the person tagged several people and then escaped back onto his side of the field, he got a point for each person he tagged. But if the offensive raider got tackled, the other team got a point. The raider had to shout, "Kabaddi!" continuously as he chased his opponents.

This particular month, there was to be a Kabaddi competition between the kids of our village and the kids of another distant village. Kabaddi was a very prestigious game, and it was very important to be victorious in the games.

"We must win," I said to Panu.

Panu looked at me as if he'd had an amazing idea. "Have you heard of Sunder Boyragi?" he said. "He's a priest from the next village. That priest knows magic. He can teach us some mantras, and then we will be able to win. One hundred percent guaranteed."

"Alright, let's do that."

When we asked the priest, he said, "Yes, I will teach you some mantras so you can win the Kabaddi competition. But you must come to me very early in the morning."

"How early?" we asked.

"Four or five in the morning."

"Okay," we agreed, scurrying off toward home.

The next morning, before dawn, we crept through the sleeping village toward the priest's house. The frogs were singing in the fields, and the insects were chirping loudly in the predawn blackness. We made our way to the priest's home. In his house, he had a small room that contained a large image of the god, Kali. He was a Kali worshiper.

"Okay, come in one by one to learn the mantras," the priest welcomed us.

The priest invited Panu to come with him, and the priest and Panu disappeared behind the goddess. Moments later, Panu rushed out of there and said, "Let's get out of here! We don't need to have any mantras. Quick! Let's go!"

Hearts pounding, we ran out of the priest's house and didn't stop until we reached the brick steps that led down to the pond. Frogs were still singing peacefully in the pond, and insects were still chirping in the darkness of the mango trees. Our hearts started to calm down.

"What happened?" I asked Panu, still startled.

"This is what happened," Panu said. "As soon as we were alone, the priest slid his hand into my genitals. I was so scared!"

Confusion covered me like a mist. Since this inappropriate action happened right behind the image of the god, why didn't the god interfere? Question after question filled my mind. I started thinking, "My prayers may or may not do any good. Either the priest is not telling us the truth, or the god is incapable of protecting us."

I started thinking that something was very wrong with the rituals that I'd been accustomed to.

A few days passed by. Panu and I didn't talk much about the priest's behavior, especially not the sexual implications. It was too disturbing and confusing for us to understand.

"We will not tell our parents or anyone else what happened," Panu decided.

"No one would believe us anyway," I agreed.

"We will not tell anyone, even our friends," Panu repeated.

One day, two priests stopped by our house for a routine visit. One of them was the one who had touched Panu inappropriately. As usual, my mother, aunt Mamima, grandmother, Jyoti Mama and I had to line up to bow our heads and touch our feet. One by one, everyone bowed. When it was my turn, my mother looked at me. Urgently, she gestured to me, signaling that I should perform the rituals.

But in that moment, I made a brave decision: *I won't do it.* I never imagined I would be able to ignore my mother's order. But I did.

"Gopal," my mother screamed. "You must be ashamed of yourself. Go inside. I will teach you a lesson."

After a severe punishment, I was resting in my room. That evening, my grandmother asked me, "Why were you so defiant?"

Slowly and steadily, I began to confide in her. After I told her what happened, she looked at me for a long time. Then she gently hugged me and uttered in a soft voice, "Don't worry, I will take care of it. You don't need to talk to your mother."

I didn't know what she told my mother. But I do know

that after that day, my mother never asked me to line up for those occasional rituals.

Realizing that my grandmother was willing to stand up to these customs and rituals gave me the courage to ask out loud some other questions that had been bothering me. So one day, I boldly asked my mother, "Do you feel that was the right thing to get married at nine?"

"What?"

"Weren't you married when you were just a child?"

"Whatever god does is well-intended," she replied with resignation.

It still didn't seem okay to me. There were things that god supposedly intended that just couldn't be right. To burn a house down with a mother and baby inside it, just because of village superstition; this could not possibly be the will of god.

The environment I had grown up in was so disciplinary that everything had rule and law. There were unwritten codes of conduct that we could not go beyond. In the village, if an elder punished us children, we could not come back and tell our mothers, "This guy hit me," because she would support the elder unconditionally. "You must have done something wrong," she would say. This only made village life worse. Children had no recourse. We didn't have a voice or a way to complain about mistreatment. Everything in the village was contaminated; there was no cleanliness. Villagers lived in the same despairing resignation that my mother displayed: "Whatever happens, happens."

As I pondered these things, my childhood faith seemed to crumble. My love of my religious rituals was deeply shaken. What the priest had done shook my life. I felt deeply disillusioned with my faith, and that confusion and disillusionment never left me.

Not only was I shattered on the inside, but the tremors of outside societal change which we'd barely noticed in our insulated village, were becoming so severe that we would soon be forced to stop and pay attention.

PART II

GROWING PAINS

9

WORLD WAR II

It's not quite true to say there had been no hints of violence in our secluded area. Even in our isolated village, we started getting vibes of World War II. Our country looked favorably on Hitler since he had joined Japan in fighting against the British rulers who controlled India. We also saw Hitler and Mussolini in a positive light. People would compliment a handsome young man, "You look like Hitler. You look like Mussolini." No one would say, "You talk like Churchill."

In December 1942, when I was four years old, the first signs of disruption filtered into our isolated village. That winter morning, Mother tucked me in my warm *chadar*, a thick, hand-woven piece of cloth. She wrapped it around my little body and tied the ends behind my back. Most mothers used this clever method to make sure that the *chadar* stayed tucked closely around their kids' bodies while they ran and played.

When I was almost ready, Panu hopped in from his

house. Even though he was only two years older than I was, he was responsible enough to take care of me. At least that's what my mother believed.

As we headed towards the village square at the edge of the pond in the center of the village, a few other kids joined us. Like every winter, an aura of golden fog hung over the pond, glowing in the morning sun. This fog had a pleasant, earthy smell. Particles of rich, healthy soil hung in the cool, moist air like a pleasant blanket of gold. As we walked toward the pond, we collected small branches and twigs to start a fire so we could share the heat during the nail-biting cold.

As we walked toward the pond, we suddenly heard a weird humming sound coming from the sky above. Our other relatives heard it too. They came out of their houses, eager to find out what it was.

"It is like a swarm of birds flying over us!" Panu shouted.

"But they are not birds, their wings are not flapping!" I replied.

"We are witnessing a miraculous phenomenon of flying objects!"

With intense curiosity, Panu and I rushed to the village square at the pond site to meet our other friends.

"Did you see what we saw?"

"Yes!"

"What was it?"

"I don't know!"

Everyone had witnessed the phenomenon, but they did not have any explanation. Later in my life, I came to unravel what happened that day. Japanese fighter planes were flying over our village in broad daylight to reach Kolkata, a hundred miles away from our village. As a colony of the British empire, India was being dragged into an unwanted war and forced to become a part of the Allied Forces during the second world war.

In early 1942, the Japanese were rapidly advancing through Asia, and the British army stopped their advance on the borders of India. Kolkata, because of its proximity to Burma, was an important target of the military operation of the Axis Force, composed of Germany, Japan and Italy.

By May 1942, the Japanese defeated the British troops and felt that Kolkata was well within their reach. The entire city was declared under curfew. On the 28th of December 1942, the imperial Japanese army bombarded Kolkata. The Japanese fighter planes were attempting to bring destruction to one of the crown jewels of the British colony Kolkata, a spot that fell under the jurisdiction of the Allied army, composed of Great Britain, France, the United States, the Soviet Union, and China. The target was to destroy the Howrah bridge, which was newly commissioned, and the seaports located nearby.

As far as I know, the Japanese could not destroy the Howrah bridge. However, they were successful in creating panic amongst the residents of the state of Bengal. They dropped as many as 130 bombs in and around the city, three sorties in December 1942 and one in January 1943. Over 70 bombs were dropped over the dock area and the casualties on that day were nearly 500.

At the time, I knew none of this history. I did not know

that our country was involved in three major conflicts. First, there was the external conflict we were dragged into because of World War II. Second, there was also an internal conflict with the British. Leaders of the Indian Independence Movement were attempting to gain independence from the British, some through nonviolent means and some by violent means. Finally, there was a very personal conflict between the Muslims and the Hindus in India, a smoldering spark that would leap into flame with the exit of the British from India.

But I knew none of this in my insulated village. I only knew that because of the bombing, my father came home from Kolkata. Before that year, the only things I knew about my father came from the stories my mother and grandmother told and the unique gadgets that he sent us from Kolkata. Whenever Dad sent a gift, my mother would show it off to the neighbors. One such gift was a flashlight. When mother pressed a button, the light came out. Both of us gasped in amazement. This was so much better than a kerosene lamp, which had to be cleaned, trimmed, and filled every morning. The daily ritual of cleaning the kerosene lamps had always fascinated me; I watched my uncle Mama and aunt Mamima moving from lamp to lamp, cleaning and filling them and making sure they worked. But this lamp was automatic, no cleaning necessary! I reached for it in awe.

"Do not touch it," Mother warned as she stowed the flashlight away.

Previously, all I knew of my father was the amazing gadgets he sent. But now, after the bombing in Kolkata, I got to see my father with my own eyes. Awe filled me as I gazed at him. My father was very slim, a little taller than my mother. His complexion was fair. Because of British rule, we all yearned for fair complexions. At a young age, I was fair-skinned, but my father and mother were both fairer than I was. Father was very vibrant and slim, with Mongolian and Chinese features. He had a long face and a sharp, European nose. When I saw him, I was scared and amazed.

"O my, he is a living human being," I thought. "He is my father!"

Perhaps I'd seen him before, but this was the first time I had ever realized he was my father. As a three- or four-year-old, I had thought I didn't have a father. Now, I was excited to realize, "I have a father, just like everyone else! And he's handsome!"

Father was a very reserved human being, but I could feel his love when he hugged me. He was a short, slender man in his forties. He had a piercing pair of eyes and wore rolled gold-framed glasses. He also had a well-trimmed mustache. His shiny black hair was parted in the middle. Above all, he had the fairest complexion I had ever seen in the village. Fairer than Panu, fairer than my mother. No wonder villagers called him Podder Sahib!

Father added an affectionate twist to my nickname, calling me Gopla instead of Gopal. The endearment felt inviting and sweet. As he hugged me, he said, "The most important thing in life is to get educated. If you don't get educated, you'll be stuck in this village, measuring and weighing grain. That will be your life."

·   ·   ·

Now that my father was home, life seemed to glow like the morning sun on the mist. A horde of young people joined my father in returning to the village after the bombings. Since our village school only educated children up to grade six, most young men went away to Kolkata and other cities to be educated. They stayed in Kolkata after graduation to work, coming home only for summer vacation or Durga Puja. But now, they came in droves after the bombing.

These vibrant young people threw themselves into drama and acting. Once a year, drama teams would come to our area and retell important stories of our history. My father became involved in the upcoming production, and I was given a part in the play. One of the characters in the drama, the Muslim emperor, had two small children, and I was to be one of the children.

In the story, the emperor was fighting with his enemies, who were portrayed as surprisingly similar to the British. Nowadays, every drama had a way of sneakily speaking out against the tyranny of British rule. The poets and actors had to be subtle, so they didn't get caught and executed by our British rulers, but they used the regular religious drama events as venues to slip in anti-British sentiment. They cleverly modified traditional Hindu songs and music to incorporate political themes. Traditional religious stories suddenly became infused with anti-British concepts.

For example, in the Ramayana ballad, where Rama fought his enemy Ravana and tried to rescue his wife, the song began to imply that Ravana's army was composed of barbaric, white savages, comparing them subtly with the British Army. "The white men are barbaric, uncivilized savages who eat raw foods," the ballad implied. "We must defeat these uncivilized men!"

In the Indian Independence Movement, there were some very clever poets and actors, and dramatists that induced an anti-white, British movement within the retelling of traditional scriptures. One of these political poets was Mukunda Das, a poet who influenced the Indian Independence Movement. He depicted the antagonists as British, and he intertwined this message very effectively into the traditional story.

As I practiced my lines and performed my parts, my love for drama was ignited. I began to understand the power of art, film, and poetry to create social change. These dramas gave me a creative outlet, provided new things to imagine, and offered me a different perspective for viewing village life. Plus, they gave me something interesting to do. Most of the time, nothing interesting happened in the village. We woke up, walked to school, came back, ate, gathered with friends, and goofed off. There were no organized activities. But this drama ignited the power of my imagination. I would need this power of imagination many times in the future to envision a better life and overcome my adversity. Through my power of imagination, I began to believe: If I can imagine it, I can do it.

I was going to need my ability to overcome adversity. One night, I lay on my bed, tossing and turning. Beneath me, the coconut husks crunched inside my mattress. I couldn't sleep. A few days ago, I'd had a fistfight with one of my friends, Bhola. It seemed like any other fistfight, and

I hadn't thought much of it. But today, Bhola had suddenly died of cholera.

"I shouldn't have done that," I thought. "I shouldn't have fought him. Now I will never be able to play with him again! He's gone!"

And he wasn't the only friend who was dying. Nearly twenty-five percent of my friends were dying, dropping like flies. Life was no longer smooth in the village. I realized for the first time how very vulnerable I was.

"It's a famine," my grandmother explained when I asked her why so many of the villagers were dying.

But this did not make sense to me. There was just as much rain as ever. The crops were growing. Why were we dying of hunger? In our insulated village, none of us fully understood the reason for the 1943 famine. Later, I understood that during World War II, Winston Churchill decided to divert Indian food supplies to his well-stocked army, rather than allowing needy villagers to enjoy the fruits of their hard labor. It was his policies that created the manmade famine.

All around me, villagers were begging. One day, I saw a very old woman begging for food. My mother and grandmother's teaching sprang to my mind: "He who serves any living being serves god."

"Here, come with me to my house," I told the old woman. When we arrived at my home, I ran inside. "Mother, Grandmother, come quickly! There is an old lady who needs food."

"Gladly we will feed her," my grandmother replied.

"Gopal, you are a wonderful young boy. Thank you for helping this old lady."

As food shortages increased, people started eating whatever they could find, even things that were unsanitary. The resulting cholera outbreak killed thousands of the population. In total, the Bengal famine killed an estimated three million people. Yet as people died from starvation all around us, I noticed that my paternal uncle Jathamosai's *godown* (storage shed) was packed full of rice.

"Why is he hoarding when people are dying?" I wondered. "Outwardly, he is so pious. It makes no sense. What a contradiction. What hypocrisy."

Though my uncle's actions were not compassionate, I later realized they were somewhat understandable. Churchill was stockpiling food for his troops in case of a Japanese invasion. He exported food from India to his British troops in the Middle East. And he co-opted Indian modes of transportation, such as boats, elephants, and carts. Without their boats and carts, fishermen were not able to bring in food for their families and the entire community. Commerce was disrupted. Famine ensued.[1]

As a result, many villagers reacted by hoarding. Like my uncle, people wanted to save their precious resources from being stolen by the British. Prices inflated. Food was scarce. As a result, millions died.[2]

There were only a few bright spots in the bleak scene of death. During the *ashtaprahar* celebration, people chanted, "*Sri Krishna Chaityana, Prabhu Nityananda, Hare Krishna hare Ram Shree Radhe Gobinda,*" for twenty-four hours straight. With the help of local women, the village priests cooked vegetarian items, including dhal, rice, and mixed vegetables. They prepared a huge feast for a couple hundred people. All the ingredients for the food were provided by our paternal uncle, Jathamosai. Then they distributed food to the poor villagers, an event called Mahotsab. There was still some compassion in existence, somewhere in the world.

10

———

THE WONDERS OF KOLKATA

By 1945, at the end of my fifth-grade year, things seemed to be looking up. In Sagarkandi, we received news that my brother Borda was getting married in January 1946. His arranged marriage would take place in Kolakopa in Dhaka, which was the village of his wife-to-be. They would then return to Kolkata for a reception. My father was throwing a party for Borda. He was inviting my sister-in-law's family, along with anyone my father wanted to invite to Kolkata.

Shortly before the wedding, I headed for Kolkata for the very first time. My mother stayed in the village because my sister Bina was too young to come along. With my father, I set out walking across the rich and fertile river valley of the Padma River, which flows from the Himalayas to the Bay of Bengal. Dozens of little tributaries cut through the marshy fields. Potholes full of water dotted the plains. The natural water reservoirs snaked their way past lush rice fields, providing natural irrigation. This river valley was all I had

89

ever known. But I was about to be dazzled by a whole new world.

The Padma was a treacherous river that must be crossed by boat in order to get to the train station. These small boats often capsized on their way across, but nobody seemed to care much. "Oh well, a few people died," people shrugged. Life in the village was a mess.

After we crossed the river, we trekked to the nearest railway station. Sitting on a bench by the station, my heart started pounding in my chest. A giant black steam engine was headed our way. I'd never seen anything like it in my entire life.

Even now I can almost smell the coal dust mixed with vapor, condensing and falling on my face. The smoky smell filled my lungs as I breathed deeply in awe. The train chugged closer and closer.

"How can it move when it's so big?" It blew my mind. I had no idea that such a monster could exist.

The train car was very crowded. It was full of different kinds of people, bringing wares from their village. People carried their possessions in bundles made of flat pieces of cloth. They would open up the cloth, dump stuff on it, tie it, and make it into a *potla,* a sack. There were no nylon or polycarbonate suitcases; the only kind of suitcases available was made of tin, a sheet of steel coated with other material.

We rode for over eight hours in the packed, smelly train car, the 140 miles from Sagarkandi to Kolkata. But I barely noticed. I was in a dream. I watched out the window in utter amazement. I counted every station we went past.

Finally, I saw the biggest railway station approaching in

front of us. The Sealdah station was a massive brick building with countless peaked roofs and graceful metal arches over its windows. I couldn't believe my eyes. In every direction, railroad tracks converged upon the station. This was a main junction railway station, one of the biggest in Kolkata.

When I got out of the train car, everything looked surprising. I had never seen so many people in my life. In the village, we all knew each other; each face was a friend, a neighbor, or a relative. But here, everyone was a stranger. I could hardly imagine that so many total strangers could exist.

"Is everywhere like this?" I wondered.

As I walked out of the station, I felt like I was in a fantasy land. There were big black automobiles, their giant spats swooping down over their wheels. There were trams. I had never seen anything like it before.

In a daze, I hopped into the phaeton, a lightweight horse-drawn carriage. I settled myself into the comfortable leather seats, mounted atop huge yellow wheels with long, spidery spokes. I could hardly believe what was happening. As the graceful black horses leaped forward, the fancy carriage seemed to soar along the paved roads.

I didn't know then that the phaeton was named for the mythical "Phaethon, son of Helius, who nearly set the earth on fire while attempting to drive the chariot of the Sun."[1] I didn't know that the phaeton is "both fast and dangerous," or that a famous poet, Thomas Warwick, had been "thrown to his death" from a Phaeton in the 1780s.[2] All I knew was that I felt a powerful mixture of awe and fear as we sped along the roads. I clung to the side of the carriage, hoping I did not fall out.

As we drove, I was captivated by the paved roads. The streets were coated with asphalt made of bitumen and sand. A layer of crushed stones and bricks was mixed with petroleum byproducts as a binder, then covered with a layer of pitch. It was the same substance used to temporarily patch streets in America. It had the strong smell of hot asphalt and pitch.

My mind began to fill with questions. "How did they make these well-organized roads? In my village, there are just dirt roads."

Kolkata was a clean city. The paved roads were washed by water from the nearby River Ganges. Once in a while, you would notice cows and stray dogs wandering around. It was very warm and humid, just like in the village.

As our carriage rolled down the paved streets, I saw stores everywhere. I had never seen shops like this before. In my village, there was only one place to buy things: the bazaar. We drove past huge brick houses, each brick cemented to the next with concrete. The houses were two, three, or four stories tall with flat concrete roofs. I was speechless.

"This is heaven," I thought. "After I finish my sixth-grade education in the village, I will come back here to Kolkata."

When we arrived at my father's house, I was stunned to see that he also lived in a three-story brick building. But when we got inside, I was surprised to realize that he only rented one room. Many other renters shared the building.

There was a common toilet in a separate area, and we had to walk to it. There were three to four tenants on each floor, and we shared two toilets and no showers.

The days raced by, and my brother, Borda's wedding reception arrived. Sumptuous foods were spread out in my father's home. Guests rotated through our home in three or four shifts, and we attended each group and made sure they enjoyed themselves.

The first course was a heap of steaming white rice with melted ghee, salt on the side, and hot green pepper. Then we served rich golden dhal, a soup with lentils or legumes. With it, our guests ate cooked vegetables and potato or eggplant fries. After that came the main course of fish. There were three types of fish: carp, shellfish, and shrimp. We usually ate the same four courses at home, but we usually only had one type of fish. But today was special. It was a feast like no other.

After the fish, we served dessert: delicious, homemade pudding made of rice and condensed milk. We passed out the regional sweets of Bengal. Just like every area of India is famous for its sweets, Bengal is famous for its cheese-based desserts. The White Sandwich was a delicate white dessert made of rich buffalo-milk cheese. Bright yellow Chandrakala was made of homemade cheese, jelly, and milk. Rosogulla was a cheese ball cooked in sugar syrup. And the Golap Jamun was a dark brown ball made of curdled cheese stuffed with the aromatic floral taste of saffron.

Paan was the last course, which was served after the guests were finished eating. Paan was a betel leaf wrapped around a mixture of chopped betel nut, calcium-hydroxide lime, and bright red paste, which is extracted from acacia wood. Guests ate paan after dinner to help with digestion. To wrap up the festivities, we offered the guests a complementary cigarette to smoke after the meal. In a whirl of bright garlands, colorful garments, and delicious foods, the party came to an end. The last wisp of smoke from the cigarettes faded into the evening air.

Kolkata had thoroughly impressed me and whisked me off my feet. I was captivated, already dreaming about my plans to come back and continue my education. I often found myself wondering which career path I'd take in life.

"What will I become? An engineer, a lawyer, or a doctor? Medicine is interesting; I'm a science-oriented guy. But really, any education that gives me a chance at a better life is a good choice."

One day shortly after his wedding, my brother Borda had a question for me.

"Do you want to go and see the hospital where I work?" he asked. My brother was interning at the RG Kar hospital in Kolkata.

"Sure," I said. I was curious.

When we filed into the hospital, I was overwhelmed by the noise and odor. Twenty beds crowded into one room. Patients were crying, yelling, and moaning. Very few nurses seemed to be available to attend the patients. The medicine was scarce. The place was not well managed. I saw amputees getting treatment for their bandaged, bleeding stumps.

For days afterward, the mental images of the hospital kept coming back to my mind.

"I'm never, ever going to become a doctor," I vowed. "I will have to try something different... like engineering."

One day while we were in Kolkata for the wedding, there was a knock at the door. When we opened it, we saw my father's next-door neighbor, a doctor. His face was glowing with astonishment and joy.

"Good news!" he shouted to my father. "Your son Chorda came in fourth place out of twenty thousand students in Bengal!" He was referencing Chorda, my second oldest brother, who had been finishing high school and matriculation tests in another district. In the test my brother had recently taken, there had been thousands of students in Bengal competing for top placement. According to these tests, my brother was fourth best out of twenty thousand. "Your son came in fourth place in the nation!" the neighbor repeated, gasping in astonishment. "Your son is a miracle. He has accomplished a miracle! His name is in all the newspapers."

My father and I were elated. At that time, we had no way to foresee that Chorda would go on to get a master's degree in Nuclear Physics and a Ph.D. in Molecular Biology. Later in life, he would become the vice chancellor of Kolkata University and a member of the Parliament in the Indian Government. But even then, we knew that Chorda was the North Star of the family, the one we all should follow.

"Wow," I thought. "One of my brothers is a doctor, and the other one has become famous in West Bengal overnight.

I want to be like them. After this wedding season is over, I will go back to Sagarkandi and finish sixth grade. Then I will come back to Kolkata and continue my education as my brothers did." In the back of my mind, there was another thought. "I can get out of the village and its superstition through education."

I loved the village, but deep doubts had begun to plague me about our rituals and beliefs. In Kolkata, I saw a whole new world opening up to me: a world that was not controlled by rituals, rules, and superstition. But I would soon discover that even Kolkata was not as free from deep religious conflict and confusion as I had hoped.

11

HUMAN MADNESS

"While kings fight amongst kings, plebeians die."

"Rajai rajai juddho kore, ulu khagra prane more."

— *A BENGALI FOLK PROVERB*

In July or August, my new sister-in-law's family invited me to be a chaperone for Boudi, my brother's new wife. According to Hindu ritual custom, a new bride goes to visit her family for a few days when the wedding is complete.

"Would you like to be my chaperone?" she asked me. "You can accompany me as I go visit my uncle on Nimtola Ghat street. It's only a mile away from your father's home."

I eagerly agreed. Only seven years older than I was, Boudi felt like an older sister. Together, we headed to her uncle's apartment building on Nimtola Ghat street.

Nimtola Ghat street was a wide street that led directly down to the riverbank. At the bank, there was a *ghat*, which are concrete steps that lead down into the river. There, the famous Nimtola Crematorium sprawled along the banks of the river. It was a famous place where people could cremate their loved ones. Funeral attendants known as *dom*, who were untouchables because of their occupation, would build a pyre of wood logs. The body, which was covered in a wealth of white and orange flower blossoms and drenched generously in ghee, was offered by the priest during the Last Rituals. The *dom* then placed the body on the pyre. As the pyre burned, the mourners walked clockwise around the fire, chanting, "*Ram nam satya hai.*" ("God is the truth.") The priest chanted appropriate mantras, expressing his wishes that the soul would reach heaven. It took about three or four hours for a body to burn. The *dom* allowed the fire to burn itself out. As the body was transformed to ashes, we believed the soul was released to heaven. Then the burnt fragments of bones and ashes were thrown into the Ganges.

Later, electric crematorium ovens would join the wooden pyres at the bank of the river. My own father, mother, and brother Chorda would one day be cremated there.

But I wasn't thinking about death that day in 1946 when I went with Boudi to her uncle's house. The house was on the main street, one of the major thoroughfares of Kolkata. Like most houses in Kolkata, the building was full of rooms that were rented by individuals. There were four rooms on each floor, and we were staying on the second floor.

One day in August, we were sitting on the roof of

Boudi's uncle's two-story house, enjoying the morning cloudy sky. In India, roofs were a favorite gathering place. During summer, people would lay their mats on the roof to sleep. It was a favorite place for throwing parties, drying clothes, or just gossiping in the afternoon. Today, we noticed that a procession was forming on the major street below. Though we didn't know it yet, the groups of rioters were parading down several major streets of Kolkata, converging at the Monument, a tall, pale yellow tower a long walk away from Boudi's uncle's house. Though the monument was not visible from Nimtola Street, it was the location of the protest.

At the time, I didn't fully understand that the protestors were demonstrating in favor of a Muslim homeland. The British had finally announced that they were going to grant India independence, and preparations were being made. The British still hoped they could keep India united, and not partition it between Hindus and Muslims.[1] As British representatives discussed the technicalities of transferring power to an independent India, tensions grew between the All-India Muslim League and the secular, inclusive Indian National Congress. While the Indian Congress wanted to be respectful to all religions, the Muslim League was built on a long history of slowly-growing misinformation between the Hindus and Muslims. To oppose them, the Hindu Mahasava party was formed. As tension built, the Muslim League requested and demanded a land to themselves, apart from the Hindu majority of India. The British debated with the Muslim and Hindu rulers of India, and hard feelings continued to intensify. Hindu and Muslim newspapers stirred up antagonism with their inflammatory statements.[2]

Finally, a Muslim leader named Muhammed Ali Jinnah decided to take action himself. He refused the British suggestion to pass the government to a combined Hindu and Muslim government. Instead, he said he had "chalked out a plan" and was "preparing to launch a struggle."[3] He threatened "that if the Muslims were not granted a separate Pakistan then they would launch 'direct action.'"[4]

The leader of the Muslim League, Huseyn Suhrawardy, asked the governor of Bengal to declare an official holiday on August 16. The governor agreed, closing government buildings in preparation for the riots. But a leader of the Hindu Congress Party asked Hindu shopkeepers not to close their businesses. Tension was rising as the rioters began to parade toward the tall white monument ten minutes from the house where we were staying.

The rioters didn't seem completely peaceful. People started throwing brickbats and stones. Others carried iron bars and bamboo poles. At the meeting, 100,000 Muslims gathered to listen to inspirational speeches. Chief Minister Suhrawardy explained to listeners that he had taken care of the police, which seemed to imply that his listeners were free to do whatever they wanted to the hapless Hindus around them. As the meeting dispersed, chaos ensued down our street. Muslims began breaking into Hindu shops and attacking Hindus with bottles and bricks.[5]

"Akhand Hindustan (United India)," shouted the Hindu Mahasava on the street below us.[6]

"Muslim homeland," screamed the Muslims, charging forward with iron bars, swords, and whatever implements they could find.

I sat frozen on the roof, watching the riot happening below us. I couldn't take my eyes off the horrific scene down below. Everywhere around me, people were screaming. There was so much blood. Not only were people killing others, but they were brutally dismembering them.[7]

I spotted an older teen from Boudi's uncle's apartment building running into the street to join in the commotion. As a hockey player, he wielded a field hockey stick that curled up at the end like an inverted candy cane. As he moved through the crowd, this innocent boy turned into a monster. He started killing people with his hockey stick. For a moment, I shielded my eyes. How could I watch our own neighbors killing and being killed!?

The scene made me sick, but I could hardly take my eyes away. In our Hindu-dominated area, the Hindus were so angry they thought it was okay to kill any Muslim they could find. The victims seemed so helpless.

"How could they do this?" I thought. "How can they feel such violent emotions? Why are these people killing?" Personally, I had no such animosity. To me, the killings seemed senseless.

As the day stretched into evening, dread filled me. If I went out on the street, I would be killed. I couldn't go back home. I was stuck here with Boudi and her uncle. I couldn't see my father. What was I going to do?

Worst of all, my newly-married brother was stuck in the hospital where he was doing his internship. He was in a Muslim-dominated area where Muslims were attacking Hindus. My brother could very likely be killed.

The killings were even worse the next day. Over the course of a week, between five thousand and ten thousand people died. It was one of the greatest genocides that ever happened in the history of the world.[8]

After a few days, the killings subsided. I hurried back to my father's Kolkata residence, a mile from Boudi's uncle's home. There, my father was unraveling at the seams. People were getting killed left and right, and he was deeply concerned about my brothers.

"They're dead, I'm sure of it," he moaned.

It didn't help that every day, we heard rumors.

"Oh, in that part of the city, all Hindus were killed."

"In that area, all Muslims were killed."

This nearly drove my father to insanity. He became incredibly unstable.

"I don't know if my sons are still alive," he wailed.

My sisters, who had been living with my brothers and father in Kolkata, were hysterical.

"Probably my brother is also killed," they sobbed.

The days of worrying about my brother were a living hell. These heartbreaking memories of the mindless killing would stick with me for the rest of my life.

In order to understand what brought about this tragic day, and the horrific violence that would follow and eventually force me out of my childhood home forever, it's important to take a step back and review the history of India.

12

BROKEN INDIA

Dear Nayan,

You may wonder why I have to give this back-drop to tell the story of my village life. Do history and current events really matter that much? That's what I wondered when I was still living in the village. The village was completely isolated and immune from the world affairs and Indian politics of that time. The village was self-sustaining with little outside support. No matter what was going on in the world around us, we felt safe, stable, and secure in our isolated haven. We didn't think that current events could affect us.

But in reality, the outside activities finally impacted the entire village, ending up in chaos and mass exodus. So I will give a very condensed version of the twenty years of Indian politics and international events that impacted our lives before 1947.

The year was 1931.

India's revolutionary thinker and leader was named

Subhash Chandra Bose. His goal was to free India from the British and create "complete freedom… with a classless society."[1] Unlike peaceful Gandhi, Bose said, "I am convinced that if we do desire freedom we must be prepared to wade through blood."[2]

There were also many other individuals who played a major role in India's independence. Many people of India still debate over which player was most significant in the Indian Independence Movement. Some debate in favor of revolutionaries like Subhash Chandra, Surjya Sen, Khudiram Bose, and Bal Gangadhar Tilak, while others say Mahatma Gandhi and the nonviolence movement were the most influential.

In 1931, Subhash Chandra Bose was carefully observing the situation in Europe while Adolf Hitler of Germany started making the military advances that would start World War II. Later, Hitler initiated the execution of the Jews living in Germany and joined hands with Benito Mussolini, another dictator.

Subhash Chandra Bose traveled through European countries and gained political support from other countries for his goal of freeing India. Meanwhile, Mahatma Gandhi had similar goals and very different methods. Gandhi aimed to set India free from the British, create peace between Hindus and Muslims, improve conditions for the untouchables, and help India become financially and socially self-sustaining—all with nonviolent means.[3]

Bose left India in 1931 while Mahatma Gandhi was attending British Round Table conferences from 1931 to 32. These peace conferences were an attempt to conciliate differences between Indian Freedom Fighters and the British government. They were intended to be peaceful, but they accomplished little. Gandhi realized no positive outcomes from that drummed-up meeting.

Instead, the British cleverly started adapting its infamous Divide and Rule policy using the most divisive proven tools of religious fundamentalism. To isolate Mahatma Gandhi from his peaceful followers, he was arrested and thrown into jail. In 1932, British Prime Minister Ramsay MacDonald granted a separate electorate for Muslims, Sikhs, Christians, Jews, and Hindus.

The British were succeeding at dividing India once again. The act of proposing a different electorate for different religions was an act of division. In protest, Gandhi started a fast unto death inside his jail cell at Yerwada Jail in Pune. Since his movement also aimed to end caste separation and to stand up for the lowest in society, Gandhi explained that his fast was "a god-given opportunity that has come to me to offer my life as a final sacrifice to the downtrodden."[4] Six days later, the British reversed their decision. In 1935, the British raj made a new law that finally granted protection to the Muslim minority, giving them separate electorates.

Far beyond the Mediterranean Sea, Hitler became a new name of power in Nazi Germany. He started violating the treaty of Versailles, which had been signed to end World War I in March 1938.

In 1938, Netaji Subhash Chandra Bose came back to India. He accepted the nomination as Congress President and stood for self-governance and full independence of

India. He advocated using force if necessary against the British Raj. This made Mahatma Gandhi uncomfortable and led to conflict between Subhash Bose and Mahatma Gandhi. Subhash Bose wanted one centralized leadership to rule India. He wanted India to build an army of her own. Due to stark differences with Mahatma Gandhi, Bose resigned from Congress.

By 1938, Hitler had become even more powerful. No European power opposed him when he invaded Poland, Denmark, and Norway. His army won battle after battle using great army tactics. The European countries could not tolerate him anymore and declared war on Germany.

Winston Churchill became the new Prime Minister of England. Hitler tried to make peace with England, but Winston Churchill was unwilling to listen to anything from Hitler. By the beginning of September 1940, Great Britain was ready for war. Hitler declared war against the British, and WWII ensued.

Britain announced that Indian troops would take part in World War II without discussing it with the Indian Congress. He recruited 2.5 million Indians to the British army to fight on various fields. It was the most significant volunteer force in world history. It included tanks, artillery, and airborne forces.

Subhash Bose did not like the idea of Indian soldiers fighting for British rulers of India, and he formed the Indian Nation Army. Meanwhile, Mahatma Gandhi pursued the non-violent Quit India movement.

To avoid the wrath of the British Empire, Subhash Bose fled to Germany. He met Hitler and organized an army of

4500 people against the British raj. "The enemy of your enemy is your friend," he preached, referring to Hitler. He asked Indian troops not to fight for the British, but to instead fight against the British and help India in gaining true independence.

The British took a violent approach towards the Quit India movement. They imprisoned Congress leaders en masse, including Mahatma Gandhi and his wife. His wife later died in prison. The British released Gandhi because they did not want him to die, fearing a massive uprising.

The tide of WWII turned for the Allied Forces. Hitler committed suicide by shooting himself on April 13, 1945, when German forces surrendered before the Soviet Union. Japan also had to surrender, as it was fighting alongside Germany. The Indian National Army, led by Subhash Bose, was dismantled. Soon after, an unfortunate plane crash was reported to have killed Netaji Subhash. However, his death remains unexplained. His body was not found at the crash site.

The second world war severely damaged the economy of England, along with the political and military power of the British empire. They were aware that after the war, Indians would begin a broader and more aggressive movement for independence. Without the resources to continue to rule the province of India, they began considering granting India its independence.

It was against this backdrop that the riots broke out in Kolkata. Muslims wanted the British to partition India between the Muslim state of Pakistan and the Hindu state of India. The partitions would also affect Bengal, where I grew up. Hindus wanted a united India, and this was the main reason that the rioters were fighting to the death.

Prior to British partition-instigated politics, people from both religions had lived in harmony for hundreds of years. But suddenly, after the 1940s, the split between religious sects became violently worse. Indian leaders began trying to get more people on their side. The Muslim and Hindu leaders were playing games with this explosive religious situation. And the result was a brutal destruction of human life: the Kolkata Killings.

There are differing reports as to who was at fault in the Kolkata Riots. Some say Suhrawardy incited violence through the Muslim League, and Hindus were simply fighting in self-defense. Others say Hindus plotted to victimize the poor Muslims in Kolkata.[5] Because Bengal has intentionally deleted this event from its official public history, it's up to individuals, like me, to discuss my memories of this heartbreaking testimony to the power of human hate.[6]

After the riots, there seemed to be no possibility of negotiating a peaceful, united India. Hindu leaders, while hoping for unity, did not agree with the idea of a Muslim majority rule. Kolkata at the time had a 55% Muslim majority. The discussions would no longer center around *whether* to partition India, but *how* and *where*.[7]

By 1946, the British released all political prisoners and opened an independence discussion with the Indian National Congress. In 1947, the British government passed the Indian Independence Act, which laid out a timeline for the British to leave India. Rather than acknowledging the growing tension between Muslims and Hindus that had formed during the time of British occupation, the British placed their focus on leaving the country right on time—whether or not the tensions had been resolved. For those who wanted a peaceful transition, time was running out. They had five weeks.[8]

A team was created to draw the borders, but the British leader, Sir Cyril Radcliffe, had never even been to India. The British did not want to bring in experts to help with drawing the borders, since that would not only delay the process but also imply a lack of British competency. The Indian representatives on the team had practically no say. Frustrated by the heat and humidity, Radcliffe was in a hurry to finish the job.[9]

When he finally finished drawing the boundary lines, giving little consideration to the Hindus who would be stranded on the Muslim side and the Muslims who would be stranded on the Hindu side, Radcliffe decided not to announce the boundaries until after Independence Day. The British would slink out of the country and let the Indians deal with the fallout.[10]

On the 14th of August 1947, the Muslim state of Pakistan gained independence, and on the 15th, independence was given to the rest of Hindu India. Muhammad Ali Jinnah, who was the leader of the Muslim League, accepted the partition with many other prominent leaders, including Jawaharlal Nehru and Sarder Patel. Despite the acceptance of leaders, many villagers were left scrambling to deal with the practical implications of the partition. Pritika Chowdhry explains the depth of the suffering that the partition caused:

"Over 20 million people were displaced in the Partition of India in 1947… Over 300,000 women were abducted and raped during the 1947 communal violence, on both sides of the border… [Yet] 'the full extent of the forced migrations and the mass rapes have been difficult to quantify because accurate data gathering was very difficult in the chaos of those times. As many victims and refugees that were counted, there are probably as many or more that were never counted.'"[11]

My home in Bengal was specifically affected by the partition. Before the partition, a small section on the western edge of undivided Bengal had been populated primarily by Hindus, while the eastern section was primarily populated by Muslims.[12] However, the British divided Bengal some-what arbitrarily, leaving many Muslims stuck on the Hindu side and Hindus on the Muslim side. We became stranded in the Muslim-majority East Bengal. This decision and division would change our lives forever.

13

UPROOTED

A few months after the devastating Kolkata riots, I sat on the banks of the pond in Sagarkandi, soaking in the beauty of the golden winter mist. It felt so good to be back in my village after so many months away. A week after the riot, we had finally gotten word that my brothers were alive, and we had been reunited with them. At the end of 1947, we'd returned to Sagarkandi for another wedding feast with our village community. After the feast, Boudi and Borda stayed in Sagarkandi to practice medicine in our village dispensary, as they had been planning all along. They lived in the long room on the side of our L-shaped house.

When we arrived home, there was excitement in the village.

"We are independent!" they shouted. "India has gained its independence from the British."

I wasn't old enough to truly understand what this would mean for me. Instead, I was focused on the normal concerns

III

of a young boy: playing with my friends, hanging out at the pond, passing sixth grade, and taking my final grade school exams. As far as I was concerned, I was ready for life to return to normal.

But things were far from normal. For one thing, there was a completely different family dynamic in my home. My father had stayed behind in Kolkata, and my brother Borda had been assigned to be my caretaker and guardian. Borda had his own ideas about how village affairs and attire should be handled. He had been gone since sixth grade, and he was out of touch with the village way of life. Everything about our culture seemed to annoy him.

"Why does nobody in this village wear shoes or even sandals?" he shouted. "Why does everyone go barefoot? It's humiliating! From now on, Robin, you will always wear shoes to go to school."

Even though Borda felt humiliated by seeing me go barefoot, I felt humiliated by wearing shoes. I didn't want to be different from all the other children at school, and I definitely didn't want all my classmates to pick on me for wearing shoes. I reluctantly put on the shoes that Borda gave me. But on my way to school, I paused at a little swamp with a cluster of bamboo stalks. Looking this way and that, I quickly took off my shoes and hid them among the bamboo. On my way home from school, I found my shoes, put them on, and came back into the village.

Finally, Borda had had enough.

"I can't stay in this village," he said about a year after arriving in Sagarkandi. "This village is so backward!"

I was grateful to see him go. As my guardian, my brother tortured me with his ruthless supervision.

"My uncle is a doctor at a tea plantation," Borda continued. Tea plantations were owned by British landlords and managed by British people. Each 5000-acre plantation had its own doctor who cared for the hundreds of workers picking tea leaves. "He has arranged for me to become a doctor on a tea plantation."

I was grateful my brother was going away, but I would miss my sister-in-law. She was only a few years older than I was, and we had become very close. We made so many memories together, and when she left, I missed her greatly.

Other people were moving out of the village as well. Our Hindu relatives were exchanging their properties with Muslim families in Hindu India. Muslims were moving into Muslim East Bengal, and Hindus were moving out. Since our village fell in East Bengal, now part of Muslim Pakistan, the Pakistani and Indian governments had reached an agreement to allow citizens to exchange properties. If we wanted to, we could exchange our property with a Muslim who was stuck in Hindu West Bengal, now part of India, so he could come to live in Muslim East Bengal, now part of Pakistan.

Our uncles and other relatives discussed these things as they smoked their hookahs in the *outhouse*. This time, I was old enough to listen in on their conversations.

"I found a property to exchange," said my father's elder brother, who lived next door. "We are going to bring a Muslim family and we are going to move to the Bengal side." Then he looked at my father. "Are you going to move, too?"

"This is not going to be forever," my father said. "Bengal is going to get united again. Don't worry about all these things."

But one day, we heard the news: "The Muslim army is coming!"

In the middle of 1948, neither the Muslims nor the Hindus of Bengal were extremists or fundamentalists. But the Muslims from the west of Pakistan were fundamentalists and were threatening to take over the newly formed state of Pakistan.

"The Muslim soldiers from West Pakistan are moving into our village!" said the distressed villagers. "They are killing people randomly!"

For shelter, we all ran onto the premises of the Zamindar, the main Hindu landlord. His home had a six-foot metal fence and was made of brick, rather than mud. I sighed with relief as I saw the Zamindar's small army of bodyguards, armed with spears and double-barrel guns. Here, I felt safe.

As we huddled together in the Zamindar's home, I looked around me. Despite the tensions in our nation, both Hindus and Muslims were hiding together.

"None of us like the idea of the rude Muslim army coming from West Pakistan," I thought. "If only all of us could live together in harmony and peace as we have for so many years."

Then one of the ladies gasped. "I forgot my jewelry!" she said. "In all the excitement, I left it behind! I forgot it when I was fleeing!" Then she looked straight at me. "You, little Gopal, you have to go to my house and get my ornament box."

"Where is it?" I asked her.

"On the veranda! I left it on the veranda of my house!"

I jumped up to go get the old lady's jewelry, and I could hear the mocking laughter of the others.

"You are going to lose your life," they said. "You are going to lose everything. Why do you care about that lady's little bucket of ornaments?"

But I darted out of the Zamindar's house, past his tall, metal fence, out into the village, and to the old lady's house. I found her jewelry box still sitting on the veranda. I returned it to her in safety, and she was very grateful.

In the end, the Muslim army rumor turned out to be a hoax. We were relieved, and we were able to return to our home. At the same time, we realized that the situation in the village was becoming more and more untenable, politically, religiously, and culturally.

In 1949, my father decided it was time to leave Sagarkandi forever. The night before we left, I had the vivid experience of collecting mangoes from a tree that was uprooted during the violent storm. I stood on the back veranda of our *outhouse*, thinking, "My god, I have to leave this forever. How will I survive?"

That morning, as we walked across the Padma river valley, there was a lump in my throat. This might be the last time I saw those lush fields, crisscrossed with rivulets and streams. This might be the last time I paddled across my beloved River Padma. As we climbed on the train on the other side of the river, heading for a new life in

Kolkata, the reality sank into my heart like a brick in the Padma:

I was leaving my home forever.

When our train pulled into Kolkata, confusing emotions swirled through my mind and heart. I remembered arriving in Kolkata for my brother's wedding, just a few short years before. At that time, Kolkata was the place of my dreams. It was like heaven to me, a dream world of possibility. But now, I'd become jaded. The ruthless murders between Hindus and Muslims, the reality of being forced out of my home by religious conflict—these stressors were taking a toll on me. This time, I was entering Kolkata as a refugee.

The first time I came to Kolkata, I'd been struck by the affluence of my surroundings: the fancy carriages, the cars, the trams, the paved roads. And it was true, there was affluence in Kolkata. My father rented a room in a rich house built by a Zamindar family. The well-to-do family rented the first and second floors, and they lived on the top story.

But even though we were living in a big house built by a rich Zamindar family, the house was surrounded by slums. Unlike in America, where entire neighborhoods are fairly homogeneous, the rich and poor in Kolkata had to coexist side by side. This was the charm and curse of Kolkata. There were no posh neighborhoods, gated communities full of fancy houses. Instead, there were tall, rich houses surrounded by lean-tos and shacks. And I began to realize that even though there were rich houses here and there, we lived in a poorer, older area of Kolkata.

It quickly began to sink in that our family was not rich. We didn't even have water most of the day. In Kolkata, the Calcutta Corporation managed the water lines. They only allowed us to use water before 10 a.m. and for a few hours in the evening. Because of the artificial water scarcity, we kids would join the elderly at the Ganges River, where we would wade into the water to bathe. There would be a whole crowd of us, pouring water over our heads with our hands, lathering our dark hair, and dunking to rinse ourselves. It was so different from my village back home, where we always had plenty of water from the well.

I began to realize we were lower middle class, educated but poor. Our entire family lived in one small room. Even though he was well-educated, my father was not making much money at the bank. He was trying to provide for all his children with his one income, and we were feeling the pinch—literally. We were cramped into one twelve-foot by sixteen-foot room. My father, mother, sister, myself, and sometimes my brothers had to live, sleep, and even cook inside our tiny dwelling place.

Everything was so different in our dense, highly populated area. The shock was difficult to get used to. Since we were accustomed to having two spacious kitchens, several bedrooms, and other outbuildings, it was hard to be trapped in just one room.

Because we were confined to a small space, I spent most of my time outside. But when I went outside, I was shocked by the sterility of my surroundings. There was no yard for me to play in, no rich garden, no lush rice fields, and no pond with golden mist hanging over it. There weren't even any trees. Just drab concrete. The front of our apartment building was only a few feet away from the street. Only a narrow footpath separated the front of my house from the street. So as soon as I left the house, I was on the street.

And that is where I spent the next few years of my life: on the street. In those days, there were only one or two automobiles in the entire area. Mainly, rickshaws transported people to and from their daily engagements. So I'd run out on the street with the other children, and we'd play marbles and soccer.

I darted down the narrow alleyways, chasing the ball with my nimble brown feet. Chipped paint covered the brick of the buildings that towered above me, interspersed with sheet metal and shacks, colorful flags and banners. Rickshaws, with their worn wheels and leather covers, tried to get past us as their human operators pulled them down the road.

There was a tangle of legs as other friends darted in to intercept the ball. Then with one deft kick, I sent the ball into the area we had designated as a goal. There was cheering all around. Finally, I was beginning to find my place among my friends.

14

BECOMING STREET SMART

At first, I didn't pay much attention to the fact that my friends formed three distinct classes: slum kids, business owners' kids, and rich kids. The slum kids were children of the exploited lower class, including milkmen, day laborers, servants, maids, cooks, small grocers, hawkers, the underemployed, including women forced into prostitution. They lived in the lean-tos and shacks around me. Most of their parents did not send them to school. On the other hand, the business owners' kids went to grade school. Their parents were shopkeepers. When they finished ninth or tenth grade, their parents pulled them out of school and put them to work in their businesses. This class of people made good money in their shops, but they were not very educated. The third group of friends was both educated and affluent. Their parents were professional people like my father: doctors, lawyers, and engineers. These parents wanted their kids to excel in school.

As I observed the dynamics between the poor and the

rich, I became very street-smart. But my dad warned me not to play with slum kids.

"You need to get educated. I don't want you to hang out with children who don't value education. If I ever see you meeting with the slum kids, I'm going to kill you."

But just like all the other children in the neighborhood whose parents warned them not to play with people from other classes, I paid no attention to his warnings. Dad shook his head in dismay, but then he finally conceded, "As long as you go to school."

I went to school every day. Our school was a giant, three-story building at the point of the V where two streets intersected a third major street. With its bronze-colored wrought iron balconies, its barred windows, and its huge iron retractable gate, it was so different from our small village school back home. The folding iron gate led into the compound, and once we got inside, the gate was closed and locked. We were trapped inside a moldy, stuffy building, with doors and windows that never opened. It was like we were in jail.

Inside the building, several hundred students milled around noisily in their individual classrooms, waiting for the teacher to arrive. For the first time, I had to rotate from classroom to classroom based on subject. Students from grades seven to ten studied to prepare for the decisive tenth-grade tests that would determine their futures. Only a few made it past tenth grade into intermediate college. When the teacher arrived in the classroom, the room settled down a little bit. The students knew they would get beaten if they continued to be so noisy.

At lunchtime, we were still not set free. Mother had given me a few cents to buy a midday snack, so I joined the milling crowd of children by the retractable gate out front. I could smell the Indian snacks that vendors were selling on the street corner. Because three major streets intersected at this corner, there was a lot of hubbub and commotion. Lots of people and rickshaws crowded each other as they made their way past honking buses, trams, and public transportation. It was so noisy. I wished I was home in my quiet village bedroom, listening to the lowing of the cows and the singing of the insects.

At 3:30 p.m., we were finally allowed to go home for dinner. As I walked slowly down the street one day after school, several months after we began school in Kolkata, I realized that my head ached. I dragged my feet over the pavement and sighed as the day replayed in my mind.

When I had tried to answer a question in school, kids had noticed my Bengali accent.

"Bangal," they jeered, using a word that was derogatory like the n-word. The residents of Kolkata were called "Ghotie," but we were called "Bangal." After the mass migration into Kolkata, the kids got a kick out of ridiculing the newcomers. Underneath the childish bullying was a serious problem that began in 1947. Before the Indian Independence, Kolkata housed around two million people. But in two or three short years, an additional two million refugees arrived in and around Kolkata. These refugees had been displaced by the Muslim-Hindu conflict and the redrawn borders. As the refugees arrived, the population in Kolkata doubled, and resources became scarce. Some of the internally displaced people had relatives in Kolkata that they could move in with, like my family. But most became destitute. With such an influx of residents, it was difficult to find work.

Out of desperation, people began taking illegal possession of the vacant land outside Kolkata, building temporary shelters there. Refugee camps sprang up in and around Kolkata. Sanitation became a challenge. Everything was a mess. The beautiful city became filthy almost overnight.

As a result, the previous citizens of Kolkata began to resent the newcomers. They felt that these aliens were invading their city. They were scared that the refugees would take possession of their property. They worried that the newcomers would take away all the available jobs. Because these immigrants had a different accent, it was easy for schoolchildren to pick on them and take out their anger and frustration on their innocent classmates. Though I didn't know it at the time, there was a serious problem beneath the bullying on the schoolyard. But that didn't make it any easier for me to handle from day to day.

"Here in Kolkata, no one likes me," I thought. "In the village, I was the center of attention. Everyone said I was so smart. I used to be #1 in my class, the best of the best. My father was brilliant. My brother placed number four among twenty thousand students. My uncle and brother became doctors. In the village, our family was the best family. But here, I am nothing. I am a small fish in a big pond. I am the scum of the earth. They hate us refugees. Everything is different here."

I kicked a small pebble that rattled against a metal

garbage can. I knew I was intelligent, and I had made friends with a few of the rich kids whose parents were highly motivated professionals like my father. They were impressed with my good brains, and they spread the word to the slum kids and the business owners' kids: "Robin is very, very smart." I started getting respect from the entire neighborhood. But my reputation for being smart hadn't lasted long.

Even though I was smart, I didn't work very hard at my studies. I didn't have the motivation and drive I would have needed to become a very good student. Little by little, I was realizing that I was not keeping up with this intelligent group of students. Now, as I neared my street, I saw my slum friends playing cricket with a large wooden stick.

"It's more fun with the slum kids and the kids of the shopkeepers than with the rich kids," I said to myself. "I may not be good at school, but I am good at other things. I am good at bullying. I am going to show people that I am not less than they are."

As I joined in the game of cricket, one of the local slum kids got in my way.

"*Khankir Bachha*," I insulted him. The word meant "son of a prostitute," and it wasn't inaccurate—he really was the son of a prostitute. As time went on, I added more and more curse words to my vocabulary. The better I became at fist-fighting, shoving, and cursing, the more the slum kids and shopkeepers' kids respected and looked up to me–not for my brains but for my bravery. I started becoming a hooligan leader in the student community. I could hit somebody or curse somebody like nobody's business.

One day, one of my friend's relatives complained to him that their landlord was mistreating their family.

"I will go with you and your relative to the landlord's house," I told my friend.

When we arrived and knocked at the door, the landlord's kid came out. Filled with vengeance, we began punching him in the nose, pummeling him until his nose broke. The boy howled in pain and clutched his nose with his hand. Blood spurted out between his fingers and stained his shirt.

His mother was close behind.

"You good-for-nothing children," she screamed at us. "We will file a lawsuit against you!"

"Will they really file a lawsuit?" I asked my friend as we raced down the narrow streets toward home.

"I don't know," his relative said. "They are landowners. Maybe they will."

"There is a man at my gymnasium who knows a lawyer," I said. "Maybe he can help us."

The independence movement in India had encouraged young men to frequent the gym so they could be strong and healthy in the fight for independence. I had gotten into the habit of going to the gym at the corner of the Children's Park, and I had met a man who had a network and knew a lawyer. It would be our only recourse if the landlord sued us.

Sure enough, the lawsuit was filed. I hurried to the gym owner, who accompanied us to the lawyer.

"Remember to keep quiet," the gym owner reminded us. "Don't say anything until he asks."

I nodded.

He went on, "His name is Radhika Nath Singha. He is the best defense lawyer in North Calcutta. Be careful."

We entered his office. I saw a grumpy old man sitting behind his desk. He must have been in his sixties, with a big swooping mustache covering his lips. His coarse, tangled white hair looked like it had not been combed in a long time. His white eyebrows were long and rowdy, as if he had never cared to trim them.

Suddenly, a husky voice came through his mouth, under his pulsating mustache: "What do you want?"

We explained what had happened.

"Please defend them," the gymnasium manager begged, and the lawyer agreed.

At court, I trembled in my seat. The lawyer started his defense.

"Sir," he told the judge, "is our society returning to the time of Nero? While Rome was burning, Nero was playing an instrument. Look at what happened when this child got injured. His parents just stood by and let it happen! This young kid came down from his apartment and fought with two little kids, still young enough to be in school. One of them broke his nose, while his father did nothing. How could the father stand there and not do anything?"

The judge nodded. "Case closed," he said. "These kids can go free."

"That was close," I whispered to my friend as we sped out of the courtroom.

But this close call didn't keep us from exacting retribution for other small injustices in our apartment building. In the rented house we were living in, there was another family whose kid never stopped tattling on us.

He would say, "If you do anything, I'm going to complain to your father."

One day, I grumbled to one of my friends, "Who does that kid think he is? He thinks that just because he lives in the same house, he can complain to my father about anything we do!"

"We will put a stop to his behavior!" my friends agreed.

So one day, three or four friends and I ganged up on him. We grabbed him, dragged him into a room, and shut him inside.

"Why do you tattle on us?" we demanded, our eyes boring into the frightened child. "What's your problem?"

"You're our hostage," another member of the group told him. "We've kidnapped you!"

The child was trembling. One of the guys in my group got a razor blade and began to shave off part of the kid's hair.

"Go ahead. You can go home, but don't ever tattle on us ever again," we said as we shoved him out the door and let him go free. "Don't ever come back and tell our parents we are the bad kids."

15

A MISADVENTURE

As a child, I started hearing whispers. Whispers that some rich people kept concubines. And whispers that many lower-class men went to the Red-Light district just ten minutes away from my house.

Sonagachi. It was a word that was never spoken aloud. The Sonagachi district housed around 16,000 sex workers,[1] but because the women were economically dependent and culturally conditioned, everyone pretended that they did not know that this was going on. Everything was swept under the rug.

I heard the hushed rumors that some of my new friends' fathers and grandfathers frequented the Sonagachi district. We didn't talk about it openly, but I began to understand that many people thought it was okay to go to a prostitute. Children my age were not even allowed to walk through the district, so even though Sonagachi piqued my interest, I thought I would never be able to satisfy the mysteries of this secret, sordid curiosity.

Until one day of intense, festering boredom. That day, my friends and I were standing on the stone pavement near the bank of the Hoogly River. Most of my friends were slum kids, but there were a few business owner kids with me that day as well. The warm, humid air hovered putrid around us, and there was nothing to do.

We'd already used up our typical go-to modes of entertainment. We'd come down to the Hooghly River, the branch of the Ganges that cut Kolkata in half. We'd loitered in the narrow, paved border that edged the river, smoking cigarettes on the cement railing. Then we'd jumped from the elegant cement barrier into the shining waters twenty feet below.

We'd spent the afternoon diving, splashing and swimming the one and a half miles across the river. We'd even ridden in front of the ferry that transported people from one side of the Hooghly to the other. We swam in front of the steamer, and using the momentum of the boat, we put up our hands and let it carry us across the river. Pressed against the front of the steamer, standing up in the water from the waist up, we rode like that across the river. Then we swam back and hopped into the steamer on its way back.

But now, we were profoundly bored. There was nothing to do. Suddenly, one of our friends had an idea.

"Let's venture into the Sonagachi district," someone suggested.

It seemed like a good way to entertain ourselves on that sultry afternoon. We climbed off the paved river-bank, clambered up the tree-lined incline that led to the rest of the city, and walked down Beniatola street, the street where we lived that wound up and away from the Ganges. After a fifteen-minute walk, we arrived at Sonagachi.

Inside the district, multi-story brothels towered above us, hugging the narrow alleys.[2] The buildings were blue, green, and pink, yet they were in terrible disrepair. All around us were bright market stalls. Prostitutes, dressed in bright red and yellow saris, stood at the doors to their homes, applying makeup in colorful mirrors. Some were teenagers, and others were in their seventies. Their long, black hair was loose or gathered into a sleek braid.

The prostitutes stared at us with narrow, suspicious eyes. Then one of them started ridiculing us.

"Hey, do you have big enough *things* to put inside of us?"

The others joined in, laughing brusquely as they stared at us. Embarrassment flooded our faces.

Just then, we saw men in khaki uniforms. They had whistles on strings around their necks, khaki shorts, and knee-high socks and boots. In their hands, they carried a small stick called a *betan*.

"Police!" my friend hissed.

Police sometimes showed up in the Sonagachi district, either to keep order or to respond to a specific call. This particular day, we had no idea why they showed up or who had called them. All we knew was that they were walking up the street, right toward us.

"We've got to get out of here! We are not supposed to be in this area! We are the only kids here!"

"If we get caught, our life is over."

We started running down a narrow alleyway between the

towering brothels. We felt like we were running through a "confusing, colorful maze."[3] My Roman sandals flapped against my bare soles as my feet pounded the pavement. I looked behind me to make sure the police were not following. Suddenly, I stumbled. My sandals flew off my feet. I had no time to turn around and get them.

When we were safely out of the Sonagachi district, we looked at each other with equal measures of fear, elation, and awe.

"That was close!" we gasped, clutching our chests in pure exhaustion.

Later that evening, I limped into my Beniatola house, barefoot.

"Father, I need new shoes," I said.

"What happened to your old shoes?"

"I don't know where my shoes are. I have no idea!"

There was no way I was going to tell him that I left my shoes behind in the Sonagachi district!

16

DREAMING OF UTOPIA

The kids from the slums became my best friends. Most of them never went to school; they just hung around and helped their parents with their occupations. We would go to the bank of the Ganges every day and smoke cigarettes, which could be bought individually at a local shop. When we scrounged up a bit of money, we bought one cigarette and shared it. As time passed, I identified more closely with the slum kids than with anyone else.

One day, my father and I went to the bazaar, a huge outdoor market that was open year-round. It was a hot summer afternoon. When the temperatures soared in Kolkata, the sticky black bitumen on the asphalt street began to melt. When I stepped on it, my sandal got stuck in the tar. As I walked to the market in the blazing sun, I was careful not to step on the stickiest sections. It was like a child playing a game of not stepping on hot lava… except in my case, the hot tar would really trap me if I stepped in it.

After we picked out some fresh fruits and vegetables, I

was relieved to head back home. Even though the stuffy room we shared was hot, it at least provided shelter from the burning sun. But when we got inside and my father began laying out the vegetables, he gasped.

"I forgot to pay that guy who we bought this vegetable from! You have to go back to that booth and pay that guy. Here are a couple of quarters to pay him."

I groaned inwardly. "We can pay tomorrow," I said.

"No. Go now and pay him now. Tell him that I am sorry."

I snatched up the coins. Frustration filled me as I made my way down the sticky street, trying to avoid getting stuck. Sweat trickled down the back of my neck.

"What would be the problem if I just went tomorrow? I don't understand the meaning of my father's decision."

As I continued walking, my anger boiled like the bubbling tar on the street.

"How is Dad going to make money if he is so honest? Why couldn't he just keep those coins? We need them more than the vendor does!"

I yanked my foot out of the sticky tar and continued to ponder. When I was back in the village, I had thought of my father with a dreamy, idealistic fervor. I viewed him as affluent, idyllic, almost king-like. But now I realized that he was obstinately honest, generous, and strong-minded to a fault. He stood up for his values, even when it got him nowhere financially. He sacrificed for his children, at the expense of his own welfare. He stood up for his liberal-minded commitment to India's independence, even when it meant he had to quit his law practice and get a low-paying job giving legal advice at a bank.

Every few months, my parents would host relatives in their very tiny one-room apartment. Relatives would stay for two weeks or a month. If someone from the village needed treatment in Kolkata, they would come live with us. My father and mother were so generous that they sacrificed their own well-being.

"This is never going to get us anywhere in life," I thought in despair. "Dad is highly educated, but he's not the rich person I imagined he was. What's the use of education? Dad isn't rich. He's not famous. He can't even make a good living. I don't know why I even try to be educated."

By the time I reached the market and turned back toward home, I had made my decision. All around me, people were taking bribes, stealing, and cheating. That must be the only way to get rich.

"I will have to steal to get rich," I thought.

Our first act of thievery seemed to have a good motive. On specific religious holidays, like Durga Puja and the feast days of the gods and goddesses, people would announce that they were having a food giveaway. The news spread like wildfire to the poor people of the locality. People would find out the day and the time, and they would show up for the free meal.

At that time, poverty was widespread. India had just received its independence from the British, and despite high expectations, nothing was happening. There were no jobs for the common people. There were bank jobs, government jobs, and jobs in small shops, but that was it. Even educated people were unable to find work. So when my friends and I announced that we were going to host a food giveaway for young kids, our neighbors were delighted.

There was only one small problem: we didn't have the resources to buy the food to give away. So we did what we felt we had to do: my friends and I stole rice and lentils from a nearby shopkeeper. Then we cooked rice with ghee and served sumptuous platefuls of delicious steaming rice, smooth dhal, and tasty desserts. The poor people and beggars swarmed around us, and we felt like we'd done a good deed for the world. I was trying to reconnect with the kind-hearted child I had once been, the Robin who led the old woman to my mother during the famine so that she could be fed.

"He who serves any living being serves the god," I told myself.

My second act of thievery was another attempt to reconnect with my childhood dreams. As I became more and more disillusioned with my life, my grades continued to slide. I spent more and more time doing mischief instead of studying. I started skipping school so I could go with my slum friends to the Hindi cinema. My parents prohibited me from seeing these movies, but I barely cared anymore. My family was always so strict and regimented, and the only ones who truly accepted me were these thugs and hooligans.

The Hindi cinema was not a posh movie theater. The chair backs were hard, and so were the seats. There was no air conditioning. The room was stuffy and musty because of the high humidity. But as the movie began to flicker on the screen, I sensed a deep yearning begin to reawaken.

Not only did we watch Hindi films, but we also enjoyed American western films with horse riding and gun fighting. We loved historical films, too. As I watched the storylines of The Three Musketeers and Robinhood, I was reminded of the victories of Rama as he rescued his queen. I was reminded of great heroes who overcame all odds, who rose above their circumstances.

"You can overcome all of these things," the movies seemed to speak to me.

I remembered when I had been an actor on the stage with my father and the teens from Kolkata. I remembered when I had formed my own drama team and performed in an old lady's house.

"I could become an actor," I said to myself as the film drew to a close. "I could become a movie star in Bombay."

When I got home that evening, I had to come up with clever lies about where I had been and what I had been doing. But I didn't mind. By this time, I was very good at escaping my problems. And with the idea of going to Bombay, I finally had a way to escape my entire failing life.

Through the complex push and pull of many circumstances—my rigid family, my failing grades, my newly awakened desire to become an actor, and an urge to escape my failures—my decision to escape Bombay became even firmer. I was held in the sway of my newfound dream.

"If I go to Bombay," I thought, "all my troubles will be over."

One day, I brought up the idea to my friends. "Let's go to Bombay. There are some fantastic stories about people who went there and became heroes of the films."

"We have nothing to lose," said a friend from the slums.

"Yes, let's go," said my friend from the business class.

I reiterated, "This whole thing about life sucks. Let's go to Bombay."

Then one of my friends asked the unspoken question that none of us had been brave enough to face.

"How are we going to get to Bombay?"

None of us knew the answer to this question.

"You know, one of my neighbors has lots of brass glasses and plates," one of my friends finally said. "We can steal them and sell them and make a lot of money so we can get to Bombay."

It was the best option we could think of. In the middle of the night, two of my friends climbed up on the roof of a nearby house. In that area of Kolkata, the houses were about four feet apart. By positioning themselves on a house nearby the target, my friends could take a flying leap and make it onto the house of the owner of the brass utensils. Then all they would have to do was walk down the stairs into the house, steal the items, and toss them down to me on the street below. We'd make a dash for it, and then we'd be well on our way to Kolkata before anyone suspected us of the thievery.

Quietly, my friends snuck into the house and emerged back onto the roof with their booty. I stood on the street below, ready to catch the items they threw down. We all knew that we would have to be very, very quiet. This type of thievery happened often, so the whole city slept with one ear open so they could hear the intruders. My friends couldn't shout to me to alert me when they were ready to throw down a cup or plate. I had to watch them closely. In the pale glow from the streetlight, I tried to track the falling items with my eyes and catch them silently without letting them tumble to the ground. I caught most of them. But then one brass item slipped out of my grasp and fell on the ground with a loud clatter.

In one terrible racket of brass on concrete, I knew that our chances of success were gone. Everyone in the area was alert to this kind of activity. As soon as they heard the noise, they started yelling and shouting.

"*Chor, Chor!* Thief, thief!"

Screaming people ran onto the street. Bhuto Da, the local *dada,* saw me. A *dada* was a local leader who sometimes extorted money from people in the area, but also protected them from the government and outsiders.[1]

"How could you do that?" Bhuto Da asked me, looking straight through me. "It makes sense that the slum kids would do something like this. But you? How could you do that? Your father is a lawyer. Your brothers are very successful. Why did you do this? Get out of here before you get whipped like the rest of the slum kids."

I darted away from the streetlamp and through a quiet alley. I slowed my pace to a walk. I had no idea where to go or what to do. I had never contemplated what to do if my plan failed. I stopped on the street corner and weighed my options.

"What is my next step?" I thought. "If I go back home, I will get severely beaten. I can't go home. I shamed my family too much to show my face to my father. What should I do?"

I finally wandered to the nearby Children's Park, where I often went during the day to exercise at the gym. At night, it was quiet and empty. By the light of the moon, I could see the patch of grass, some of the only vegetation in Kolkata.

I sat down on a bench. Time seemed to stop. I don't know how long I sat there, thinking about my life.

"How could I have done this?" I thought bitterly. "I brought shame on my respected family. My father has made so many sacrifices for us. My mother and father are trying so hard and giving so much to give us an education."

It was several hours before my brother found me in the park and marched me home to face my father. When I glimpsed my father's face, I saw utter disgust that I had never seen in my entire life. He looked at me and nodded his head. His eyes started welling with tears. He turned his back and walked away. It was worse than a beating. I felt the unbearable pressure of my father's disbelief and dismay.

I felt tears pricking at the edges of my own eyes.

"Never again," I whispered to myself.

I'd always heard that coal is transformed into diamonds under tremendous pressure. But would the pressure in my life be enough for me to change?

17

CHANGE AGENT

The West Bengal School Final Examinations were approaching. These tests, which took place at the end of 10th grade, would determine who made it into the limited spots in the elite Indian colleges. The tests were very selective. But I was not doing the work necessary to pass them. When I failed a key class, my parents and I began to realize that I was not going to make the cut. I was not going to graduate from high school. There were only four or five months left before the final exams, and the way I was headed, it looked very unlikely that I would pass.

"You are the worst child we ever had," my mother despaired. "You're never going to shape up."

"You are not actually studying," my father realized with regret. "You are not going to school and doing what you are supposed to do. How can we remedy this situation?"

Thankfully, Father did not give up completely. He found a teacher who had taught my uncle in Kolkata. It was a last-ditch attempt to salvage my grades.

On my first day with the tutor, the teacher conversed with me for a little while and got to know me a bit. Then he cut to the chase. "Do you think you will be able to do it? Will you be able to study enough in five months to pass the test?"

I didn't say anything.

"What is your problem? You are an intelligent boy. Why can't you do well at school?"

Again, I didn't answer.

"You said you cannot do it? Why can't you do it? You are intelligent, I can see. You are good at math. Why can't you do well in the rest of the subjects?"

My teacher could see that his questions were making no impact on me. Finally, he took a different approach. He launched into a story.

"Once upon a time, there was a man named Rama whose wife, Sita, had been kidnapped. After searching for her for some time, Rama found his wife, Sita, on the island of Sri Lanka. He needed to find a way to cross the water to get to the island, and he didn't have much time."

As the teacher spoke, the childhood story seemed to flash before my eyes like a movie. In my mind, I was back in my bedroom in the village, reading by the light of the kerosene lamps. I recalled my finger moving over the lines of poetry as I read and memorized almost the entire book of Ramayana. Now, listening to the tutor, tears came to my eyes as I remembered the familiar story. Because of my love for the Ramayana, his words were profoundly meaningful to me.

"Rama had to build a bridge between Sri Lanka and

India, to cross the Arabian Sea and the Bay of Bengal. But he didn't have much time. Rama and his military force built the bridge across the sea and finished it in just five days.[1] They killed the evil kidnapper and rescued Sita. The bottom line is this: if a hanuman led military force can build a bridge in just five days, you can study for this test in just three months. If Rama could build a bridge that stretched all the way from India to Sri Lanka, you can pass this test. You are intelligent. You can do it. You just have to put your mind to it."

I nodded, deeply moved. What he was saying was true. I really did have a bright mind. It was not that I didn't understand the topics I was studying; it was just that I had developed bad study habits. And from now on, that would change.

After dinner, I opened my books and studied all through the night. From ten o'clock to six the next morning, I read and memorized fact after fact about Bengali literature, history, and geography. I took a short nap in the morning, and then I was back to work. When the tutor came, I paid close attention to what he said about math, science, and English. I tried my best to absorb the proofs, formulas, and polyatomic equations.

Finally, the week of the tests arrived. We took several three-hour tests on different subjects in our classroom at school. When I was finished, the test papers were sent to a centralized location so the results could be evaluated against 20,000 other students' results. In those days, there were no computers that could tell you the results of your exam. There was nothing I could do but wait.

One day, a friend of my father's ran into our house, out of breath. He had been to the school to check on something, and he had seen my test scores.

"Hey, I just saw on the chart that your son has passed with first division!"

Shock and surprise overwhelmed me as I overheard the man's conversation with my father.

"Can it be true? Did I really pass the tests?" As the news sank in, I realized, "Now I am finally a part of my family!"

For so many years, I had been drifting away from my family. The contrast between me and my brothers and father had been increasing every day. They were all bright, intelligent, and prosperous; I was failing. I was the wayward child, the black sheep of the family. Now, I finally felt like I was one of them.

That moment of renewed self-confidence was enough to propel me forward into engineering school. But would it be enough to get me through the confusing maze of bribery, political unrest, and betrayal that lay ahead? I'd seen people who faced life's challenges with honesty, yet never attained success. They were honest and ineffective, like my father, who despite his education remained quite poor. I'd also seen people who were dishonest and effective, like the people who bribed their way to the top. And I'd seen people like my past self, who was dishonest and ineffective: I'd been caught in the very act of stealing!

Now, in the wake of such a great reversal, I vowed to become successful, honest, *and* effective. But did I have what it took?

PART III

——

REACHING MATURITY

18

CHASING EXCELLENCE

One day after I passed my school exams, my brother gave me a note.

"Go and leave this note with the professor at Presidency College," he said, beaming at me with pride. "It is the #1 college in all of West Bengal. This note will help you get in to intermediate college."

I took the note and started off down the paved street toward that college. But as I walked, my mind was working overtime to figure out what to do.

"I don't want to go to the Presidency College," I said. "It is an all-male school. How will I ever meet a girl there? I want to go to Scottish Church College, a co-ed college. I want to meet all those girls!"

In our highly restrictive and supervised community, there were no opportunities to talk to girls. Unmarried girls and boys were not allowed to even speak to each other. A co-ed college would be a nice opportunity! By the time I had reached the tall, ivory-colored pillars of the Scottish

Church College, I had made up my mind. I turned aside through the lovely, patterned wrought iron gate of the college and applied there instead.

When I got home, I told my brother casually, "I couldn't find the gentleman you recommended. So on my way back home, I got into Scottish Church College."

On my first day of college, I headed to school in my typical outfit of shorts and a button-up shirt. Moments after I set foot on the campus, I saw the girls tittering behind their hands. I could feel their laughter. A humiliating warmth filled my face. Every man around me was dressed in full-length trousers.

When I got home, I begged Chorda, "Can I borrow a pair of trousers?" It was so awkward! The next day, I made sure I was wearing trousers. So much for making a good first impression on the girls!

These two years of college would determine my future. If I did well, I would be able to take the entrance exams for advanced college. In our intermediate college, there were only two tracks: science and literature. Those who chose literature started with liberal arts and moved on to commerce or law. Those who chose science could go on to get a bachelor's or master's degree in science to become a science teacher or professor or get into postgraduate studies like Chorda did. I chose science because I wanted to become a doctor or an engineer. If I did well in my intermediate science classes, I would have a chance to take the entrance exam and qualify for continued education in engineering or medicine.

Two years of intermediate college flew past. Without

letting my parents know, I scrounged up the fee for the exams to qualify for professional school.

"This is my chance to become a doctor or an engineer," I thought. "But this choice does not only depend on merit but is also chosen by lots. I want to try for engineering, and if I fail, I will go into medicine. I know I may not pass. I'd rather my parents didn't know—in case I fail."

But as it turned out, I was the only guy in the entire area who passed the entrance test. Now, the choice of career was up to me: I could choose between engineering and medicine. I really wanted to go into engineering to prove to my brothers I was no less than they were.

My father had been looking for jobs for me, not knowing about my test results. One day, my father said, "I'm going to take you to the bank where I work. I already talked to them, and you are going to start work as a bank clerk."

"I already took the qualifying test to become an engineer," I told my father. "I would like to continue to go to school to become an engineer."

"I can't pay for that," my father said. "I can't afford it."

My father was right to say he couldn't afford it. He made only 300 rupees per month and engineering residential school cost 125 rupees a month. Paying my tuition, room, and board would deplete 50% of my father's income. But in an act of surprising support, my entire family got together and contributed toward my school fees. All my uncles and my elder brother started pitching in. It was a big deal for my family that I got admitted into engineering school, and it seemed like a miracle to me, too. The day when I would move into the college campus was fast approaching.

It was the first day of Engineering School. The summer afternoon was hot and humid, but I couldn't care less as I looked out the window of the taxi, watching the city of Kolkata pass by. A mixture of excitement and nervousness churned in my stomach as I thought about the journey ahead.

My family had always struggled with money, and getting into the elite Bengal Engineering College (BE College) was a dream come true. I felt proud of myself, but I also knew that this was just the beginning of a long and difficult journey.

As we reached the Howrah station, the chaos of the bustling city hit me with full force. People were rushing to and fro, porters were hauling heavy loads, and taxis were honking as they darted in and out of the station.

My mother and sister made sure that I had everything I needed for my hostel stay. My mother had packed my bags with clothes and toiletries, while my sister had bought me some snacks for the journey.

"Make sure you have the mosquito nets," my sister said, handing me a small package.

"Yes, I know," I replied, rolling my eyes. "I'm not a kid anymore, *Didi*."

"If you think mosquito nets are unnecessary, just wait until you wake up on the rooftop covered in itchy red bumps," she teased, with a mischievous smile.

I couldn't help but smile at her. She grinned back. I felt grateful.

We boarded the bus to BE College, and as we crossed the iconic Howrah Bridge, I caught a glimpse of the mighty Ganges river flowing beneath us. It was a breathtaking sight, and I felt a surge of pride for my city and my heritage.

As we arrived at the campus, I felt a sense of awe and wonder. The grand buildings, sprawling lawns, and busy students all seemed to beckon me to join in the excitement. My heart was pounding with anticipation and I could hardly wait for the orientation to begin.

As we walked through the red brick buildings toward my hostel room, I couldn't help but feel a bit overwhelmed by the size of the campus. My sister-in-law noticed my apprehension and said, "Don't worry, it may seem big now, but you'll get used to it in no time. You're going to have the time of your life here!"

My brother Chorda, who had a bit more experience with college life, added, "And don't worry about anything, we've got you covered. You've got all your essentials, right?"

I nodded, feeling a sense of relief wash over me as I realized how lucky I was to have such a supportive family. "Yes, I've got everything I need."

They both smiled and assured me once again that everything would be fine. "We'll be back soon to check on you, but for now, just get some rest and prepare for tomorrow's big orientation meeting. You're going to rock it!" my sister-in-law said with a grin.

I hugged them both and watched as they left the hostel. I felt a sense of excitement and nervousness wash over me.

This was the start of a new chapter in my life, and I couldn't wait to see where it would take me.

Looking back on that day, I realize how much that journey symbolized for me. It was a journey from a low-income family to an elite institution, from the crowded streets of Kolkata to the serene campus of BE College. It was a journey of hope and ambition, of dreams and determination. And I knew that I was ready for whatever lay ahead.

I still remember the following morning, as I sat amongst the freshmen students in the enormous meeting hall of the main engineering building, waiting for the orientation meeting to start. It was 6:55 a.m. and the room was buzzing with excitement and anticipation.

And then, right on the dot, at 7:00 a.m., the door swung open and a professor walked in. He was tall and imposing, with a stern look on his face. He looked at us with a sharp gaze, as if sizing us up.

"You have to get accustomed to 7 o'clock," he said, in a deep voice that carried through the hall. "That's when the factory starts."

He paused for a moment, letting his words sink in, before continuing.

"Out of thousands of candidates, only 180 of you have been selected. You are the cream of the society and India needs you. The Central Government has just started the second five-year plan. It's you students who are going to lead us to success."

I could feel a sense of pride and responsibility wash over me as I listened to his words. The professor's voice was commanding, and his words were a call to action that I could not ignore.

He looked at us one by one, as if searching for something, before concluding, "We will push you to your limits, and we will challenge you to be the best version of yourselves. But I have no doubt that you will rise to the challenge and make us all proud."

As I left the meeting hall that day, I knew that my life had changed forever. The weight of the professor's words hung heavy on my shoulders, but they also filled me with a sense of purpose and determination. I was ready to take on the world, and I knew that I had the support of my college and my country behind me.

A couple of days passed. My course load started increasing. One moonless night, I was sitting alone, pondering my life. I was thinking about the challenges of college life and whether I was capable enough to face them. Suddenly, I heard a screaming sound. The air was thick with the sounds of chaos and excitement on the college campus. I hurried out onto the street below and stood with a group of new students, my peers.

The senior students had organized their annual ragging ritual, and the unsuspecting new students were their targets. The seniors stood outside, smoking cigarettes and laughing at the younger students as they approached. The new students were nervous, and their hearts were beating fast, but they were also excited to be part of this so-called "rite of passage."

As the new students drew closer, they were greeted with a barrage of insults and derogatory comments from the seniors. The seniors demanded that the new students sing a song or dance in front of them, or else face the consequences. The new students were hesitant, but the seniors were relentless, and they eventually gave in.

One of the seniors, a tall and imposing figure with a sneer on his face, approached a new student who was visibly trembling with fear.

"Hey, you there!" the senior barked, pointing a finger at me. "What's your name?"

"R-Robin," I stuttered.

"Come on, you bastard son of Rabindranath Tagore! It looks like you're in for a rough night," the senior said, his voice dripping with sarcasm. "Recite a poem."

The other seniors chuckled, egging their comrade on. I looked around and realized that we were completely outnumbered.

"I-I'll try," I said, in a voice barely above a whisper.

"Good," the senior said, grinning maliciously. "Because if you don't, we'll kick you in the ass. Start."

The seniors made the new students do all sorts of humiliating tasks. They were forced to crawl on all fours like dogs, eat bizarre food combinations, and drink disgusting concoctions of various liquids. The seniors even made some of the students strip down to their underwear and run around the campus, all the while being taunted and laughed at.

The ragging continued deep into the night, with the seniors becoming increasingly aggressive and cruel. We were left feeling violated and traumatized.

Surprisingly, the next day, when we met some of the seniors, they greeted us with compassion.

"Don't worry, these are the normal rituals of our college. Everyone has to go through them," said one of them.

As the days passed by, I couldn't help but notice that most of the students in my class were from affluent, elite families. They seemed to effortlessly blend in, with their expensive clothes and their confident, well-spoken manner.

I, on the other hand, was just a boy from Beniatola, coming from a poor middle-class but educated family. I felt out of place in this new world, like a fish out of water. I didn't know how to make friends with them, or how to keep my dignity intact.

I tried to keep to myself, focusing on my studies and avoiding any interaction with my classmates outside of the classroom. But no matter how hard I tried, I couldn't shake the feeling of inadequacy that gnawed at me.

One day, as I was walking back to my hostel, lost in thought, I heard someone call out my name. I turned to see one of my classmates, a tall, well-dressed boy, walking towards me with a smile on his face.

"Hey, I've been meaning to talk to you," he said, his voice friendly and open. "I noticed that you always keep to yourself, and I wanted to make sure you feel welcome here."

I was taken aback by his kindness, and for a moment, I didn't know what to say. But he didn't seem to mind, and instead, he continued to talk, telling me about himself and his family, and asking me about mine.

As we walked, I began to see him in a new light. He was

just a person, like me, with his own fears and insecurities. And in that moment, I realized that we weren't so different after all.

From that day on, I made an effort to be more open and friendly toward my classmates. I realized that there was no need to feel inferior and that my background and experiences had value. I had something to offer, and I was just as worthy of their respect as they were of mine.

I began to feel like I was truly carving out a space for myself to belong and matter. Every week, I spent Monday through Friday in the hostel with my new friends and returned home for the weekends.

Through my friends, I allowed my mind to take me to new places I'd never allowed it to go before. Through my new friends who were from socially elite families, I was introduced to thoughts, feelings, and customs I'd never experienced before. They were well-educated young people from wealthy bloodlines. Their parents and grandparents had been educated, upper-class members of society for generations. For example, one of my friends' fathers was a principal of another engineering school in another state in India. I also made friends with a guy whose father was a well-known film actor in West Bengal.

I began realizing that the world was bigger than my small, restrictive room at Beniatola in North Kolkata. My confining environment was not the only environment. There were other people out there, other ways to think about life, other perspectives, and other ways to do things. Not everybody had the same code of conduct. I caught a glimpse of the future... of freedom.

Best of all, my elite friends and conversant literary knowledge helped me impress the girls. Even though I was in a science track, I became an avid reader of literature: English authors like Shakespeare, Wordsworth, and Tennessee Williams, as well as Bengali authors like Rabindranath Tagore, Nazrul Islam, Sarat Chandra, and Bankimchandra. Being well-read and conversant in many different types of literature was important in my new circles of friends, and especially important to the girls.

But the first girl I liked was not at school. She was one of the tenants in our Beniatola apartment building. In 1953-1954, one of the tenants on the second floor of our building moved out, and my father was lucky enough to be able to rent those three additional vacant rooms.

It was like we could all breathe a sigh of relief. The financial burden on my father was easing. My brother, Chorda, had gotten scholarships, which reduced my father's expenses. Borda had become a doctor. My elder sister had gotten married. We had fewer people at home, and we also had four whole rooms and a kitchen! Life was becoming a little easier, and things were getting better and better—especially once I met Sheila on the second floor.

19

GETTING MARRIED

Sheila was a beautiful girl. Her hair was long, smooth, and dark. Her face was like a sculpture from an ancient temple.

I knew I could not talk to her; my parents were always watching, and they would never allow it. But I began to think about her day and night.

"Could I sneak out to the park?" I thought. "No, my father is so strict, and he never stops watching us. What could I do? How could I get in contact?"

Finally, I decided to write a letter to her and try to find a way to sneak it to her. With trembling hands, I penned the words, "Meet me on the path to the toilet at five in the morning next Monday morning."

Now, I only had to figure out how to get the note to her in the first place. I carried it with me in my pocket everywhere I went, hoping for a chance. Finally, the opportunity presented itself. I passed off the letter and waited for a response.

All that week at engineering school, I was trembling with excitement, anticipation, and fear. When I went home for the weekend, what would I find? On Monday morning at 5:00, would Sheila meet me? Or would I be standing alone in the predawn chill, looking like a fool?

The next Monday morning, I stood in the dark alley, my fingers numb with cold. I tried to make myself as small as possible so that no one would see me. It was risky to linger like this on my way to the bathrooms. If I stayed too long, my father would suspect me. A lone cricket was singing.

Suddenly, I thought I heard shuffling feet. A girl emerged in the darkness. Without even looking up, she pushed a small paper into my hand. Then she continued on down the path to the toilet. She knew as well as I did how risky this was.

Every Monday after that, we started meeting at five in the morning to exchange letters. We couldn't pause long enough to talk or even look each other in the eye. But Sheila handed me her letters, and I read them over and over during the week.

One day, I sat in my hostel room, the letter in my hand. But my mind was far away, on Beniatola street.

"I love you, Robin, and I always think about you." I read the words again. "Someday, we'll meet and hug each other and cuddle each other. I can't wait for this day."

Life was truly looking up. I had affluent friends, a successful career path, a more spacious home, and a love interest on the horizon. And best of all, while attending

Engineering School, I discovered a local drama group to be a part of. One day, we were preparing to perform a translation of Shakespeare's Hamlet.

"We need a Hamlet," one of my fellow actors said. "Where can we find someone tall, good-looking, and good at acting?"

"We must search the neighborhoods for a young person who wants to join our team," I said, remembering the thrill I'd gotten back in Sagarkandi when the older actors chose me to participate in their drama productions.

After some searching, we found a young man named Shelly. He was from the same neighborhood as I was, and he was great at acting.

"Shelly, join our drama group!" I begged. "We need a Hamlet who is tall and good-looking like you!"

So Shelly started rehearsing with the rest of us. I remember Shelley's magnificent performance, especially after he delivered the famous opening soliloquy of Prince Hamlet in Shakespeare's Hamlet, in the Third Act. In the speech, Hamlet contemplates death and suicide, weighing the pain and unfairness of life against the alternative, which might be worse.

The Bengali playwright who translated Shakespeare's Hamlet was Ajit Ganguly. He adapted the mid-nineteenth-century classical Bengali language to emulate the essence of the Shakespearian style. Here is a snippet of the richness of Ajit Ganguly's Bengali translation:

Hamlet:

"To be, or not to be - that is the question:

Whether 'tis nobler in the mind to suffer
The slings of arrows of outrageous fortune
Or to take arms against a sea of troubles
And by opposing, end them. ..... "

Hamlet (translated)

"Ostyitae japon, kimba nastitya bilop,
nirosoner ai to sonshoy.
Monete jantrona dai durvagyer nikhipto
ostro ar saraghat
Sreotoro ki ei jantroner bhog
Othoba bipod sagor rodhe atmonashe tader
bilupti... "

Shelly was curious about Shakespeare, and he and I enjoyed having long, intellectual discussions about literature. Because Kolkata had been the capital of all India under British domination, we were all enlightened by British influence. In engineering school, I'd had the privilege of mingling with the best brains in the country. I'd met many affluent, sophisticated classmates. To belong to those circles, I was expected to be conversant in English writers like Shakespeare, Shaw, and Virginia Wolfe. I also became familiar with Russian authors like Tolstoy and Dostoevsky and French authors like Franz Kafka and Albert Camus. Shelly enjoyed discussing these topics with me, and we soon became close friends. I even began confiding in Shelly about the girl I was falling in love with —despite the fact that falling in love was not smiled upon in our culture.

In those days, it was customary for a young man's father or eldest brother to find a middleman who would decide which family had a girl who was suited to marry the young man. The middleman would arrange for the boy and the girl to get to know each other a bit and talk to each other for a few hours under the strict supervision of the parents. Even though marriage customs were slowly changing—girls were marrying in their late teens instead of late grade school years—society still frowned upon people who married for love instead of by family arrangement. My brother Chorda had decided to marry a girl he loved; this broke my father's heart. At first I looked down on Chorda's actions. Yet now that I was falling in love myself, I could understand why someone would want to do that.

"There's a beautiful girl who lives in my apartment building," I confided in Shelly one day. "I can't stop thinking about her."

Shelly listened intently to my description. "Go on," he said.

I couldn't stop pouring out the intense feelings in my heart. "I think about her day and night. I can never talk to her, but I found a way to sneak her a letter. Now she meets me every Monday morning on her way to the outdoor bathrooms. We exchange letters."

"Robin, I am so happy for you. What does she say?"

I blushed. "She says she loves me and can't wait to marry me one day. Shelly, I've been thinking and dreaming about the day I could marry her. Do you think it's possible? Would my father allow it?"

"I don't know," Shelly said. "But it's worth asking him."

"I will ask him as soon as I finish engineering school," I said. "Just one more year."

While I waited for that day, I threw myself into art, writing, and drama. I wrote poetry and got my short stories published in the engineering school's annual magazine. I also threw myself into IPTA, the Indian People's Theatre Association. This was a political drama movement that began increasingly active in West Bengal. Its purpose was to protest the plight of the working class and the way the government mismanaged the businesspeople.

I became involved in a local branch of this movement, the *Shilpi Mon* (Artistic Mind) drama troupe. The members of our troupe all had day jobs. But in the evenings, we would get together to discuss, plan, and rehearse. On weekends, we would perform by invitation at different villages and suburbs of Kolkata.

One day, the troupe director and actor Taru Da made a statement that changed my life. He was looking over the stories and poetry I had written. Suddenly, he seemed to have a bolt of inspiration.

"Robin, what's the point of writing poetry?" he asked me bluntly. "It's not like you are going to get the Nobel Prize. Why don't you start writing drama?"

Something fluttered inside of me. "Yes," I agreed. "Maybe I should write a drama!"

Every evening, I toiled at my writing desk, penning the words to my new dramas. I wrote twelve to fifteen stage plays in my language before I wrote my ticket to fame, "Naba Taranga." Its topic was a cause I was passionate about: the exploitation of village peasants by their landlords, the Zamindars. My passion was the seed that grew into an entire drama about the revolt of peasants against their landlord.

My drama was a wild success. It was performed all over in the remote villages of West Bengal, and the villagers loved it. My childhood dreams were coming true. Not only did I have an outlet for my acting skills, but I was using drama to change the lives of the oppressed people of India.

At least once in their lifetime, every human being gets an opportunity to do something they thought they'd never get to do. For me, that opportunity came at the All-India Youth Festival of 1962. Once a year, the central government organized a dance, music, and drama festival which took place in cities across the country. Local writers and drama teams would participate; over forty groups vied for first place in this honored festival.

Today, I sat in the lavishly decorated tent, holding my breath as the judges prepared to announce the winners of the writing contest.

"First prize goes to…" There was a dramatic pause. "…Naba Taranga!"

As wild applause broke out from the thousands of people in the giant tent, I felt like I was in a dream. I made my way to the front. As the judge lay the medallion around my neck, I felt that anything was possible.

Until one day in 1963, when Shelly dropped the bomb.

"Hey Robin, do you know Sheila is getting married?"

"What?" I said.

"Yeah," he said, looking at me with sympathy in his face.

"How could she have done that!" I gasped. "She got married without even letting me know! She married someone else!"

I knew deep down in my heart that I was not rich enough for Sheila's parents to consider me a viable candidate to become her groom. I knew that the customs dictated that Sheila had to marry whoever her parents decided. But it still felt like a personal betrayal.

"Not only did Sheila's family betray me, but she also betrayed me," I said to myself. "Couldn't she have told her family how much she loved me? Surely they would have listened to her if she had spoken up. Or she could have at least told me what was going on! We could have had one last goodbye!"

But it was too late. My first love was gone, like a spark snuffed out in the cold night air.

My father hired a middleman (*ghatak*) to help me get married. The *ghatak* found two girls and arranged for me to meet them. The first one was not my type, but the second was beautiful. Her family offered us snacks and sweets on silver platters. I was excited and enraptured! They were filthy rich. But unfortunately, the family declined to proceed. My family was too poor for their liking.

After that experience, rage filled me. I was angry with myself, my parents, and my society.

"Am I just a commodity in the fish market?" I asked myself. "Why can't young people who love each other just get married, regardless of their possessions or wealth? Am I not good enough for anyone at all?"

In 1960, I graduated from engineering school at just twenty-one years old. One year before, my brother Chorda had gone to America with great fanfare to do his post-graduate work on nuclear science. After graduation, I immediately got a job as an assistant engineer at a transportation company. It was the highest-paying job I'd ever had. It was very unusual to get such a prestigious job at such a young age. I was given a car and my own personal chauffeur. As I coasted around the city in the back seat of my new car, I could tell that everyone looked up to me.

"This is the kid who used to do all sorts of mischief," people would say. "Now look how successful he is! He has a great job."

After my brother, Chorda went to America with his wife, son, and daughter to get his Ph.D., I began to dream of following in his footsteps. So I applied and got admitted into Lafayette University in Indiana, USA.

"I am also going to go to America," I told my father.

"Son, your elder brother is in America. Why don't you wait and let him come back and then you can go?"

Ever since the moment I'd been caught stealing, I had always tried to please my father. So I changed my mind.

"OK," I said. "I'm not going to go."

Days passed by, and Durga Puja arrived. After the ten days of traditional festivities had almost come to an end, the local families of Kolkata were taking part in the ritual of drinking a sacred concoction for the last day of Durga Puja. The pale green drink contained milk, cardamom, cinnamon, nuts, sugar, and a special holy herb. This herb was believed to be a miraculous plant that sprouted where amrita, the dew of life, was poured on the earth. The herb was said to be "one of the five most sacred plants on earth… [and] a guardian angel resides in its leaves."[1] According to the Atharva Veda, it was a "source of happiness," a "joy-giver" and a "liberator."[2] It sounded too good to be true, but it appeared to be just what I needed after all my disappointments. And the drink looked delicious. I took a glass in my hand and began to sip the delectable, creamy drink.

After the festivities, my friends and I started walking to the bank of the Ganges. As I walked, I felt like my tongue was turning inside out and going further and further back in my mouth. The weird sensation only continued to get worse until I felt like I was choking. I had to find an excuse to go home.

"I have to do something, it's very important," I said.

Not caring what my friends thought, I ran back home and into my room. As I lay on my bed, writhing in misery, the sensations kept growing and growing. I saw hallucinations: my sister became two-dimensional when I started eating.

"You must have drunk something," said my mother. "Did you drink Bhang Lassi?"

"Yes," I said.

I tried to go to sleep, but I felt my whole body was moving up to the ceiling. When I finally fell into a deep stupor, I slept for two days. I barely knew what was going on around me. My mother and sister didn't disturb me.

When I woke up, my mother told me what had happened. She explained that the "holy herb" was actually cannabis.

"I will never, ever taste marijuana again," I vowed. And I never have.

Three more years passed. Despite my disillusionment with girls, I knew I needed to get married and make my parents happy. In 1965, I finally told my father I was ready. The paid middleman found a match for me, Pratima. We met on the manicured lawn in front of the Temple Pareshnath Mandir. It was a park-like atmosphere, a garden with walkways where people would go for picnics and meetings.

On January 31, 1965, my father, mother, relatives, and best friend Shelly went with me to meet Pratima. Initially, I had to sit at a distance while my parents talked with Pratima and her family. However, I was able to catch a glimpse of my potential future bride. She was calm and composed. Through her eyes, she projected a small-town innocence. She was not only very beautiful but had also graduated with Honors in Bengali literature. Suddenly, it crossed my mind that she was no less attractive than Sheila had been.

"This will be good revenge on Sheila and her family," I thought.

Suddenly, my father's voice interrupted my thoughts.

"You may talk to the girl for a little while," my father and Pratima's brother agreed. I was grateful for the opportunity to get to know her a bit. I had a very important question for her.

As we walked around the park, I cut to the chase.

"Do you like drama?" I asked. "I'm pretty involved in drama."

"Yes," Pratima said.

As far as I was concerned, that settled it. We talked a bit more, and then we parted ways.

After we came home, my parents had a question for me.

"Do you think you should marry this girl?"

"Yes, I can get married to this girl," I replied. I was so accustomed to arranged marriages that I didn't have high expectations for the process.

"You will get married on February 10," my father said.

"What? That is only eleven days from now!"

"I need to jump on this opportunity. I don't want to risk having you marry someone that is not approved by the family as Chorda did."

So despite the fact that Pratima's family lived 125 miles away in Murshidabad and would have difficulty dropping everything to plan a wedding that quickly, Father arranged for our marriage to happen ten days later.

On February 10, as the priest pronounced our marriage vows and placed a pure white garland around Pratima's neck, my thoughts briefly flashed back to Sheila.

"This is so different from what I dreamed of," I thought. "Yet I know my father sacrificed so much for me. And by marrying Pratima, I am making him happy."

To comfort myself, I threw myself into drama. A few years later, when my first son was on the way, I didn't even pause my drama schedule to attend his birth. I knew he was due any day, but I was devoted to my drama group with a cult-like fervor. When my wife called to let me know that she was going to the hospital, I was in a remote village, performing.

"Thank you for letting me know," I said. "I'll check later today to see how you are."

"Aren't you coming home?" Pratima asked.

"No, I'm busy performing this drama," I said. "I have an important role. I can't get away. Through our drama, we are saving the country and saving the world. This is too important for me. I can't leave."

Later, I called to check on Pratima.

"How is Pratima? Has she had the baby or not?"

After a couple of days, I came back and found out my son had been born. My mother was cradling Rahul with tenderness and awe. There were tears in her eyes.

"This baby is Borda," she whispered with awe. My eldest brother, Borda, had died in a motorcycle accident a few months before Rahul was conceived. "This little one is your brother reincarnated," Mother crooned.

I smiled but remained silent. I suddenly realized I didn't believe in reincarnation anymore. I knew the belief helped my mother cope with the unexpected loss of her beloved son. But I also knew it wasn't true. Suddenly, I realized I was free from the superstition of the village. My scientific education had finally given me the courage to admit to myself, "This is wrong."

Education had answered so many of my questions. In that moment, I determined that I would always remain open-minded, willing to learn more about the meaning of life. I wanted to be willing to admit, "This was wrong, this was right, this is a hazy area, we have to wait and see what happens."

Meanwhile, the IPTA was becoming more and more radicalized and left-inclined. Even though India had been independent for nearly twenty years, nothing was changing. The government had gotten everyone educated, but there were still no jobs. There were thousands of educated people without jobs. The Drama Movement seemed to be our only hope for change.

And then, in 1967, my drama, "Naba Taranga" ("The New Wave") seemed to come true in real life.

20

FACING TURMOIL

"It's time for a revolution!" Charu Mazumdar announced on May 25, 1967.[1]

The Chinese had held their revolution in 1949, and the Vietnam war and Cuban revolution had recently occurred. Now, it was time for the Indian peasants to revolt.[2]

Earlier that month, the peasants in the small town of Naxalbari had decided it was time to act. For years, they had served the landowners. They had harvested the tea on the landowners' tea plantations while getting very little income for themselves. Now, they ventured into the landowners' private land and began picking the tender, juicy tea buds— and keeping them for themselves.[3]

On May 23, when the police arrived to arrest those who were stealing tea, they were surrounded by a shower of arrows. The police turned tail and ran. The movement was so unprecedented that the federal government became very concerned.

Two days later, the police tried again. When they were

once again met with opposition, the police shot and killed three local men and eight women, also killing the babies on their backs.

Mazumdar had had enough. It was time. Peasants began seizing landowners' land, attacking police stations, and killing police with bows and arrows. The Naxalites, or armed peasants, began murdering the local rich people. It was a chaotic nightmare. The left-wing parties were split, but some were sympathizers of this armed insurrection.

The government began to fight back and suppress the armed resistance. The police were on the hunt, like hungry Bengal tigers, killing people left and right. Because I had written a drama about an armed peasant revolt, I became a target. The central and local governments, as well as other opposition parties, had their eyes on me. Fear had me in its noose. I couldn't believe I had become tangled up in this whole mess.

The city of Kolkata became a nightmare, a scene of horror and agony worse than the scary ghost stories my grandmother would tell me as a child. The city would declare curfew often, trying to keep people inside and away from the police raids. But during the dead of night, the police would cordon off an area, conduct a search door to door, and pick up suspects. They would then haul them in front of the Victoria Memorial Hall Maidan.

"Run!" The police would command.

Believing they were being set free, the people would run for their lives. As they tried to escape, the police would fire at them and kill them.

After the murder, the police would fabricate a fake story

for the newspaper and radio. It was a cruel game of cat-and-mouse that brought untold fear to my heart.

Every time I was out and about in the city, terror stalked me. I didn't know whom to trust. Were my friends and contacts left-wing party members or right-wing party members? Would they sympathize and protect me, or would they turn me in to the police? Who was an informer? Who belonged to the police?

Random killings were taking place all over the city, and our beloved Master Mosai's brother had been killed. Our renowned grocer, Ganamodi, was also dead. Not too long before, my older brother Borda had died in a motorcycle accident. The fear of death was all around me. When would my turn come?

I knew I could die at any time. Though I was still a young adult, my mental stability began imploding. One night, during a random police raid, my friend from Nimu Goswami Lane was snagged, teased with freedom, then shot to death. That was the straw that broke the camel's back.

I suffered a nervous breakdown so severe that I didn't know what to do. Even when I was safe at home, I started feeling claustrophobic, like I was about to die. My heart felt like it would leap out of my chest. My feet and hands would suddenly turn cold as ice. I became disoriented, never knowing when the next attack would happen. My stomach was tied up in anxious knots, and I couldn't eat. I lost twenty pounds which I couldn't afford to lose.

"Why is this happening to me?" I wondered. "I'm not anorexic. I'm eating what I am supposed to eat." But the indigestion was so severe that I couldn't even drink water without having stomach problems.

I started researching my condition and going to as many doctors as I could. I visited any doctor I could find: homeopathic, herbal, or allopathic practitioners. None of them could tell me what was wrong. But one advised a trip to the ocean.

"You need a change of weather," he said.

At Puri, a sea resort, things started looking up. Puri was a beautiful beach town in the nearby state of Orissa. As I stood on the beach with my wife and my son, I could tell the fresh sea air was helping calm my nerves. The waves crashing on the shore and the birds circling overhead were already healing my twisted gut. Filled with hope, I returned home.

But back in Kolkata, the whole episode started again. Kolkata was a city of nightmares. Every day, there were sirens. We heard gunshots. The sound of handmade bombs ripped through the night air.

Finally, I reached a point of despair. "I'm twenty-eight years old, but I'm going to die," I said to myself. "One way or another, I'm not going to survive. Either I'll die of weight loss, or I'll die of bombs and shots."

One day, I was wandering aimlessly in the city when I came across an old friend.

"Hey," I said, my voice ecstatic.

He turned my way with a confused look. He seemed like he did not know me.

"I'm Robin," I continued, "from Scottish Church college. Don't you remember me?"

His face lit up. "Robin! Is that you? I didn't recognize you! What happened to you?"

Hesitantly, I began to recount the physical problems that had been accosting me for months.

"I just became a doctor," he said. "I will talk to my professor at RG Kar Hospital. He knows his stuff. Give me your address, and I will set up an appointment."

When I met with the seasoned doctor, he instantly diagnosed me.

"It's anxiety," he said. "There is nothing wrong with your body. It's all in your mind."

He promptly prescribed me an anti-anxiety medicine. Finally, I found some relief. But even with the anxiety medicine, life in Kolkata was unsustainable.

"Chorda, I can't stay in the city," I said to my brother one day. "There is too much pressure here! Too much danger! They are seeking my life!"

"You need to hide immediately," he said. "You can stay with me. You need to get out of Kolkata!"

My brother Chorda was living in a suburb of Kolkata with his family. I agreed to flee to his property and stay with him until I could move my wife and son to join me in my brother's house in Baguiati. But after a while of living with my brother, my wife and his wife started to tussle.

"Two women cannot live under one roof," I said to myself. "We have to find something else."

When I talked to a landowner who had the property for rent, he asked for an advance.

"Three thousand rupees," he requested.

I willingly gave it to him.

But when the time came for me to move in, the owner had news for me. "I already rented that property to someone else."

"Then give me my three thousand rupees!"

"Well, I already used them, and it will take me a while to pay you back."

"I can't rent another place without that money!"

"I have a property adjacent to my house. Why don't you buy me out."

Without a second thought, I agreed. I was such a novice; I didn't know that I couldn't build on a 32-foot by 70-foot piece of land. Everybody laughed at me because I was so naive.

"You cannot build a house on such a narrow piece of land!"

But I had a determination like steel. I went to the United States Information Services library to see if I could find a book on house engineering.

"Let me see if they have a design for this 32-feet-wide piece of land."

As I flipped through the books of drawings, blueprints, and photographs, I got some ideas about how to build the house. Because of my engineering degree, I had preliminary knowledge of civil engineering. So after a year of saving, I got together a bit of money and started building my house. When we had finished the first floor, we moved in, and as we got more money, I built it up.

People began noticing the unique architectural design.

"What an appealing house!" they would praise me. "Would you design our house, too?"

"What a great side gig!" I said to myself. Designing homes for community members provided me with some extra money, and my business was flourishing.

Yet despite the success and joy, fear was ever-present. I lost my purpose. I totally quit writing and acting. A writer must have something important to say and a platform to say it, and I realized I didn't have either. I had no venue, and I wasn't even sure if I believed the message I had been propagating. The things that I had believed in had led to violence, and I couldn't talk about these things out loud anymore. I didn't want to get involved in day-to-day politics. I didn't want to bring back the panic, heartache, and fear that I'd experienced in Kolkata. So I tried to find tasks that would take up the time and energy that I previously used for writing drama, and acting. I just wanted to keep busy. One day I thought we could start the second floor. I discussed this idea with my wife, Pratima.

She said, "That would be so nice. It's becoming a little too congested with Mother, Rahul and us."

I agreed. But I confided, "I'm seriously thinking about it. We need some additional money."

"How much."

"Maybe four thousand rupees."

She smiled. She walked up to our steel almirah and unlocked the door. She picked a small velvet sack and returned to me. She handed over her velvet sack. I pulled it open with curiosity. It was her gold bangles and few other ornaments. She said, "it's collecting dust anyway. I'd love to use it for our home. It will fetch few thousand rupees."

I became spell-bound. These are her precious gifts. I realized how deeply she accepted me and my family.

I said to myself, "I can't believe I've been so blind for so long. All these years, I've been so focused on my drama movement, everything has been about me! I've neglected the most important person in my life: my wife."

"Looking back, I realize how much she has sacrificed for me. When I was suffering from panic attacks, she stood by my side and took me to Puri to get well. When we had to hide from political turmoil, she was there, holding my hand and keeping me safe. She took care of my father, until he died in 1967. She has been taking care of my mother from the day we got married. She gave birth to our first child, Rahul, when I was saving the world far away from her in a remote village!"

"And now, she's giving up her own parental gift of gold ornaments to build a second floor for us."

"It breaks my heart to think of all the times I've taken her for granted, all the moments I failed to recognize her love and support. But now, I'm finally waking up to reality. I need her in my life, more than anything else. I want to make it up to her, to show her how much she means to me, and to never let her go."

"I know I have a long way to go, but I'm willing to do whatever it takes to be the husband she deserves. I want to love her, cherish her, and appreciate her for the rest of my life."

· · ·

We build the second floor. A little girl joined our family on July 29, 1972. We waited outside the hospital door until the doctor came out and said, "You have a daughter!"

Yet I was still not at peace.

"I have a great job, and a great marriage, yet my life is in danger," I said to myself. "Even in this peaceful suburb, I could be killed at any moment. I will either get arrested or get killed for nothing. I have not done anything that deserves death. Even if I say I'm not a part of that political group anymore, they won't believe me."

One day, in 1973 or 1974, one of my employees, an engineer, had a request for me.

"Can I get a couple of hours of leave?" he asked. "I have a chance to go to America, and I need to complete some errands to prepare my paperwork for the trip."

"Really? So you are going to the embassy, right?"

"Yeah."

Hardly pausing for air, I found the words tumbling out of me: "A long time ago, maybe ten years ago, I applied for immigration. Can you go check whether I can still go to America? Is my application still valid?"

When the engineer returned, I couldn't believe my ears.

"Yeah, you can still go. In fact, they are trying to find you to give you the news that your papers are about to expire. In one more year, they are going to discard them. They are looking for you, but since you moved from your home on Beniatola street, they don't know your address."

"What a coincidence!" I exclaimed with excitement.

As soon as I got home, I told my wife, "I want to go to America. Financially we are okay, but mentally, we are not.

There is pressure from the government. There is political pressure. I might get killed or go to jail if I stay here. And there is another source of pressure, too. My company is trying to force me to take a bribe. But I don't believe it is the right thing to do."

In my engineering job, I was a manager of 1400 people. Our organization was a self-sustained, government-funded organization responsible for public transportation for the city, Calcutta Transport Co. During the maintenance process and accident damages, we were charged with selling unsalvageable buses to the highest bidder. In our monthly meetings, the minister of transportation would talk to us about the direction our organization was going.

After one of these meetings, one of the workers of the minister of transportation had pulled me aside.

"Some people are waiting for you downstairs," he said. "Please listen to them."

Something seemed odd about the way he said it, but I followed his directions. I went downstairs and met the people who were waiting for me. I shook hands with each of them.

"Hello, I'm Robin Podder," I introduced myself. "How can I help?"

"You know that there is a tender going on," the man began. "There are a lot of bidders trying to submit bids for that bus. But I would like you to give the bus to our client—even if they don't have the highest bid."

A shadow crossed my face. Did he want me to lie? Was he trying to offer me a bribe?

"There is a lot of money involved in buying, dismantling, and selling the bus," I replied. "Whoever is the highest bidder will get the bus."

"Give the highest bid to our client," they requested, offering me a large sum of money.

"Legally, I cannot do this," I responded.

"We will pay you well," they insisted.

One day, when I'd arrived home from work, I'd seen a shiny new refrigerator in my kitchen.

"What is this?" I asked Pratima.

"A group of people dropped it off. I asked them why they were bringing it, but they said, 'Don't worry. Mr. Podder knows about it.'"

I shook my head. "It's the people who are trying to bribe me. They want to make sure they get the favor."

Now, as I talked with my wife, my thoughts swirled. "Will I sell my soul? Or will I be honest? Is it possible to be honest and successful? It's the question I've been asking myself all my life. Am I willing to take the plunge that honesty requires? If I go to America, will I be able to rebuild from the ground up?"

Out loud, I explained the situation to Pratima. "This is what happened. What do you think? Should I go to America?"

"Go," she replied simply.

I will never forget the day my chauffeur drove me to the airport. My whole family was with me, and a few Baguiati well-wishers accompanied us.

"Sir, you are going away," one of them said, pain filling his voice. "I used to watch your dramas. You used to give us so much hope. Now you are leaving us."

His tone told me that I had betrayed him. I was leaving my people to go to America. As the airplane's engines began to roar, I continued to think.

"Am I just escaping my problems? Is it worth it for honesty? I have tried so hard to be honest and successful, but all the political turmoil, bribes, and corruption have held me back. I can never reach my goal of being honest and successful while I'm in India. In India, I could only become wealthy by taking bribes. And I'm not willing to do that. The door has opened so easily for me to come to America, through what seemed like a sheer coincidence. But I don't believe it was a coincidence. Then what is it?"

As the airplane rose into the sky, I was more determined than ever to become successful *and* honest.

21

———

UNCHARTERED TERRITORY

"They worship kings only in their country, and scholars everywhere."

"Swadwshe pujjyate Raja, Bidyan sarbatra pujjyate"

— A SANSKRIT PROVERB

It was January 22, 1976, late morning. The Boeing Jumbo Jet had finally touched down on the runway of Los Angeles International Airport. I was on American soil! Mixed with the joy and relief of safely escaping Kolkata, I felt sadness. I had left behind my wife and two adorable kids through no fault of their own. As I looked around, I realized that there were only a handful of passengers who looked like me. I was a stranger in a foreign country. No one spoke my language.

The plane slowly rolled to a stop on the tarmac. Flight attendants guided us to the exit gates where the airport bus would take us to the immigration area. As we started disembarking, a new thought came into my mind. Dr. Sanyal, a student of my brother, Chorda, was going to pick me up from the airport.

"What if Dr. Sanyal can't recognize me? I've never met him before."

A few months before, when I'd met with the American Embassy personnel in Kolkata, I'd been told that all my immigration paperwork was in order. I'd updated all my personal information, and everything was good to go. However, the immigration official said I'd need to provide a $1500 cashier's check from a US resident so that I would not become a liability later on.

"Fifteen hundred dollars?" I'd silently murmured to myself. "Where the hell am I going to get that? Is this the straw that breaks the camel's back? Am I going to be told I cannot immigrate after all?" But I pretended nothing was wrong. "How soon do you need that?" I said out loud.

"As soon as possible. It's a lot of money. I'll give you six weeks. Can you handle it?" the embassy officer asked me.

"Sure," I said, as if it was not a problem at all.

Well, that was how Dr. Sanyal came into the picture. After returning to my Baguiati home, I called Chorda and explained to him what happened at the embassy.

Chorda assured me, "Let me look into it. Give me a week."

Finally, he came back to me with great news. He had

contacted a few of his friends in America and one of them, Dr. Sanyal, had agreed to send me a cashier's check. This act was only to show respect to my brother. He didn't even know me.

The immigration formalities had been processed, and I had boarded the flight two days before. By Indian time, it was the 21st of January when I arrived on American soil. But due to a time difference of twelve and a half hours, I gained a day and landed on the 22nd.

Filled with apprehension and anxiety of the unknown, I approached the arrival gate. It took more than an hour to wait in line and clear immigration and customs. I was over-whelmed by all the foreign faces. But as I was coming out through the tunnel to the main arrival area, I saw a man waving his hand, looking at me.

"This must be Dr. Sanyal!"

As I approached him, he shook my hand and said, "Call me Sanyal. How was the trip? Boy, you are a fully suited and booted gentleman. Welcome to America."

I followed him out of the airport and into his car. As he made his way into traffic, he said casually, "Los Angeles is a very big city. We live in Glendale. It will take us about forty-five minutes to reach our home."

I nodded.

"Now we are entering the freeway," Dr. Sanyal said. "Do you feel anything special?"

"Everything is special. I am amazed that so many cars are going so fast, and with no honking!"

"Well, It's not Kolkata. If you honk, you will get a traffic ticket. The cops are waiting for you."

"They will give you a ticket just for honking?" I asked.

"You bet." He then passed me a cigarette and asked, "You smoke, right?"

I nodded and accepted the cigarette, even though I was hesitant to start smoking in front of an older man. Despite my uncertainty, I lit the cigarette. Oh, what a relief. I desperately needed a nicotine fix.

As we sped down the highway, I couldn't take my eyes off the neighborhoods passing by outside the window. Everything was so clean! I had expected long rows of high-rise buildings, like what I saw in the picture of New York City. Instead, it looked more like a highly affluent village, studded with so many trees. It was not a concrete jungle like Kolkata. And besides the constant whoosh of the racing automobiles, there appeared to be pin-drop silence.

We finally reached our destination, Dr. Sanyal's apartment on Verdugo Lane. As I settled in, I noticed things were quite different here. The sofas and loveseats were bigger and wider, and they were covered with thick fabric, unlike the seats in Kolkata.

"Make yourself at home, Mr. Podder," Dr. Sanyal invited. "Put your feet up and relax. My wife Archana is at work. After work she will pick up my son and my daughter from school. They will be here soon. If you need anything, let me know." He then looked at me and said, "We have two bedrooms. One is our master bedroom and the other is for our two kids. After Archana arrives, she will let you know your sleeping arrangements."

I said, "Don't worry about it. I am very happy that I am

finally here." I was just grateful that I had been offered shelter by a stranger who had never met me.

"It is a rat race, Mr. Podder. Soon, you will figure out the charm of this goddamn country. Oh, what a country! You must be a little hungry. You relax, let me see what I can get for you until Archana returns. Would you like a cup of tea or coffee?"

"Tea would be nice. Are you going to make it?" I asked.

My face must have looked as shocked as I felt. A respectable man, making tea?

"I can wait till Misses Archana comes," I said. "You don't have to make tea for me."

He sensed the surprise on my face and startled me with his loud laughter. "You are in America now, Mr. Podder," he guffawed. "You have to do everything. Cooking, cleaning dishes and bathrooms. Doing your own laundry. You have to learn to do everything. No help from servants and maids! Nobody can afford that." Then he threw in a last sarcastic jab: "Start enjoying your American dream."

He walked into the kitchen and placed a kettle on the stove.

"Do you need milk and sugar?" he asked. "How about some cookies?"

"Cookies?" I asked.

"I'm sorry, I mean biscuits. That's the British word. Here we call 'em cookies."

As he was preparing the tea for us, I was eagerly taking mental notes about the things that were different here. Men are required to cook... Women need to work to make both ends meet… Biscuits are cookies. What would I discover next?

The next day was a Friday. In the evening, Dr. Sanyal and his family took me to a nearby Bengali party. He said, "Mr. Podder, as you can see, I am doing my postdoc in biochemistry. I have no idea how to land an engineering job. So, I'm taking you to a party where there will be a few engineers. I will introduce you to them. Unlike India, nobody can give you a job here. They can only guide you in the right direction. You will find something soon."

22

REAPING THE HARVEST

A few weeks later, I stood at the corner of Broadway and 4th street in downtown Los Angeles, watching people go by. I had hardly felt more dejected in my entire life. I had been in the United States for more than three weeks, trying to get hired. I'd attended the networking party, made new contacts, sent in applications, gone to interviews, and followed every job possibility I could find. I wasn't picky; any job was good enough for me, even if it wasn't in engineering. But I was getting nowhere. Every opportunity ended in failure.

The last few weeks had been a nightmare. Just two days after my arrival at Dr. Sanyal's residence, on a Sunday, I entered the living room and greeted Dr. Sanyal.

"I am returning your fifteen-hundred-dollar cashier's check," I said to Dr. Sanyal.

"Sit down," he invited. Then he turned to his children. "Go to your bedroom, kids."

As the children scurried off for their rooms, Mrs. Sanyal joined us and sat down on a breakfast nook chair.

"Mr. Podder, it's important to tell you now. We have decided to move back to India."

"What?" I was totally unprepared for what Dr. Sanyal had just said.

"I've been thinking about this for the last six months. It has been a difficult decision. But you know, these damn scientific institutions. They stole my work and my professor is publishing my work in his name. I have had enough. I am sorry that I had to break this news to you in this fashion. Believe me, it's killing my soul. You can stay here for a few more days. Then I will take you to a downtown motel. The city employment exchange is close by. You will find something for sure."

So I ended up in a motel. As I checked in, Dr. Sanyal handed me three hundred dollars and said, "I'm still going to be around for a few weeks. The rent is \$22 per week. I paid for four weeks of rent. I wish you the best."

After he left, I felt absolutely helpless. What the hell would I do if I failed to land a job? How could I even get back to India without any money? I had gotten a few phone numbers at the networking party Dr. Sanyal had taken me to. Worst case scenario, maybe I could beg and borrow from them.

Every day after that, I'd gone to the exchange to look for work. They had sent me to interviews, but I was not having any luck landing a job. By this time, I was totally desperate.

As I stood on a street corner, watching the people walking past on the sidewalk, I hung my head in shame.

"All these people are busy going here or there. They all have jobs, homes, and busy lives," I said to myself. "But a guy like me, who managed 1400 people back home, can't find any job at all."

One day, I met a compassionate man who seemed to sympathize with my dilemma.

"OK, I understand your situation," he said. "Why don't you come tomorrow and let me try something different."

He sent me to a job site and sent a note to the hiring manager. "If you don't select him, give me a good reason why not," he told the manager.

With his help, I landed a job as a machinist. I told the hiring manager, "I'm an engineer. I used to manage 1400 people."

He couldn't believe I could be an engineer from another country. "OK. We manufacture these heat sinks for a factory. You said you are an engineer, right? I need someone to run a drill and other machines. Can you do this?"

"Look, I did that a long time ago when I first graduated," I responded. "I had some training and I used to run a machine. This is what I used to do. I used to manage an engineering outfit."

"If you can do it, you can have a job."

I told him, "Show me how it works and I'll try it."

"You have the job," he told me when he saw my proficiency. "Ninety-nine cents per hour."

I took it.

After a month of working for this man, the owner came to me with a look of amazement on his face.

"Robin, I'm so impressed," he said. "You must be over thirty?"

"Thirty-seven," I murmured.

"Why don't you move to the quality control department where there is not as much physical labor? You will be making sure all the parts are correct."

I took the opportunity, and my pay increased from ninety-nine cents to two dollars.

Then one day, he came back to me and said, "Look, I can see that you have a very high level of knowledge and expertise. If you stay here, I cannot pay you what you are worth. I run a factory that will not allow me to pay you. I think it's time that you should look for another job. Get yourself a master's degree. That will give you the stamp of approval you need to become a qualified engineer."

It was the best advice I had ever received in my life. I enrolled in California State University and continued my study for master's. I will never forget the generous advice of that kind man.

Meanwhile, my wife, son, and new daughter were ready to join me in the United States. I had been telling my family white lies whenever they asked me how I was.

"I'm fine, everything is great," I would say.

"That's wonderful! We are coming to the United States in December," they said.

Suddenly, I was in hot water. I had found a guy from Bangladesh who was willing to split the costs of a Hollywood apartment with me. I was working my small job for two dollars an hour. But I was nowhere close to being able to sustain a family financially.

One day, as I pondered my dilemma, I was at one of the Bengali parties I liked to attend on weekends. I was chit-chatting with the people at my table. Suddenly, an important-looking man walked up.

"Hi, I work for Northrop Corporation and my name is Tapas Sinha," he said. "I used to live in Kolkata. Then I moved to England, got my degree, and got a job."

I said, "*Sinha*! Is that the same as *Singha?*"

He laughed. "Yeah, I changed it."

"I knew a Singha, Radhika Lal Singha," I replied. Then I told him the story of what happened in the court with the lawyer when I was a child.

"OMG! That lawyer is my uncle!"

"Such a coincidence!"

As we continued to build rapport, I confided in him that I didn't have a good job.

"You can't find a job?"

"No. Can you find me a job?"

"No, here in America we can't just give people a job like we can in India. But I can look to see if someone in my company has an opening."

In mid-October, when I was panicking about my wife and children coming, I got a call from him. "Northrop is looking for a facilities engineer."

"What is a facilities engineer?"

"Well, it's a kind of maintenance position that is responsible for repairing the buildings that Northrop owns."

"Well, I'm a mechanical engineer. But from building my

residential home-building business, I have some civil engineering experience."

"That is enough. That's exactly what you should say to your interviewer. Don't say you managed 1400 people and had a house and a car. Don't put everything in your resume. Just say you are an engineer and tell them about your experience." He emphasized, "There is no guarantee I can give you a job. It is not like India. You have to convince the people who are looking for that position."

With only a few months until my family arrived, I knew it was time to take a leap of faith. In a dinky little car that I barely knew how to drive, I traveled from Hollywood to Northrop for my interview.

"I will take the chance," I thought. "What do I have to lose?"

It was November the third. I can still recall the exact sentence the hiring manager told me when he called me to let me know I had been selected for the position a few days later.

"You are going to get $325."

I nodded silently. "That's about the same as my other job," I thought. "This is $325 a month, about $2 an hour."

Then the man's next words startled me out of my mind: "That's $325 a week."

I couldn't believe my ears. I nearly fell from my chair. After I hung up the phone, I sat in stunned silence for several minutes.

Then slowly, like the golden mist creeping over the pond in my village, happiness began to creep into my heart. Satisfaction filled me. I knew I had done the right thing.

"I am finally going to live a successful life," I said to myself. "I will finally be able to provide for my family. And I will do it by honest means. I will be both honest and effective. I knew it was possible if I just persevered."

And with a smile on my face, I got into the car to meet my wife and family at the airport.

Dear Nayan,

Your grandma, your uncle, and your mother landed in America on December 26, 1976.

The lesson I learned that day in America is still one of the most important lessons you can ever learn. With a strong desire to overcome, you can survive almost anything that happens to you. If you refuse to give up, and you pour your entire heart and soul into your goals and dreams, you will achieve great things.

But always, always do it with honesty.

Love,

Your Dadu

EPILOGUE

From there, my story mirrors every immigrant's story. I built myself up, got my master's degree, got a house, and watched my son and daughter grow up. We raised our kids, son Rahul and daughter Ruma, in America. Both of them are in their fifties now. They left the nest, and I welcomed my grandson, Nayan, with great love.

In 1995, I retired from an aerospace company. I retired as a manufacturing engineering manager developing technology to build both fighter and commercial aircraft. I retired financially secure at age 55. Then I went back to school at UCLA to study film structure, editing, and directing. I produced two films, "Storm in the Afternoon" and "Chosen Few." After scratching my itch for drama and writing, I decided, "I'm too old for this. I don't have the energy to work eighteen hours a day, for three years, to produce an independent film. This is for young people. No wonder actors retire early!"

In the United States, I underwent a slow cultural metamorphosis. I reexamined my way of thinking about a lot of topics, including marriage. I also faced my addiction to smoking.

In 2009, my wife and I were having a party at our friend's house. It wasn't a fancy party, just a weekend gathering of close friends. We liked to get together regularly with other immigrants who understood the challenges we faced in our new environment. Being an immigrant in a foreign country took a toll on us, and being with friends helped relieve the burden.

This party was a chance for us men to drink and for our wives to gossip. It was a noisy environment, everyone talking over someone else, discussing things that practically had no value. New jobs, new houses, new gossip about others who were not present. Killing time, but trying to have a good time. After having a few drinks, a friend offered me a cigarette. "Robin Da, please take one."

"No thanks, I quit."

Everyone guessed I must be joking or lying.

"This is your 20th time, right? That you quit."

Some giggled and some laughed out loud.

"Bullshit. You have been quitting since forever. I bet you can't quit."

Someone sympathized, "We are all trying. It's difficult. Robin Da, I bet you that you will never quit." He added, "We all know that promises are made to be broken. Right?"

Everyone burst into laughter. One of my friends asked, "How did you quit?"

I said, "Barack Obama."

I wanted to make a dramatic statement to draw everyone's attention. For me, it worked most of the time. However, it was not intentional. I guess it was a part of my innate nature.

My friend, Kamalendu, was curious. He asked, "Obama! What do you mean?"

"Well, this is what it boils down to. As you know, I've been trying and failing to quit smoking. One day just before the Presidential election, I had a family get-together. I was smoking. I was asked to go outside to finish my cigarette. Deep down, I felt humiliated.

"'When are you going to get rid of this nasty habit? It makes the entire house smell horrible,' my wife said.

"I promised my family, 'I'm going to quit if Barack Obama wins.'

"I knew deep down in my heart he would not win, because it would be almost impossible to win against John McCain. My prediction was based partly on the news media and partly on some ingrained racism. I knew Obama would not win. I made the promise so that I wouldn't have to quit. I could continue smoking, giving a lame excuse. Oh God! I didn't know a surprise was waiting for me. Barack Obama won. And because I promised in front of my wife, my daughter and my son, I told myself I had to quit. And I did."

My friends cheered for me. Through perseverance, wit, and energy, I had conquered my addiction.

Today, I live a peaceful and affluent life. My wife Pratima and I live in an old house with a large backyard. We have lots of fruit trees and my wife has a beautiful vegetable garden. She is known for her green thumb.

Our house is so close to the Pacific Ocean that I can walk to the shore. I love water, and I think it's my destiny to live near it. I went from living on the bank of the Padma to living on the bank of the Ganges, and now near the shore of the Pacific Ocean.

My wife and I have been living in this house in Torrance, Los Angeles, California, since 1983. This house has four bedrooms, a living room, a family room, a kitchen, and two baths. Glancing around my present surroundings, I am amazed to realize that almost all the stuff we take for granted and think we cannot live without did not exist in my village. There were no utilities: no electricity, no gas, no running water, and no automobiles.

In the computer room where I penned this manuscript, we have my desktop and my wife's desktop computer, two iPads, a laser printer, a couple of shelves, a sofa set, a bunch of plastic containers, a television set on a credenza, the landline and iPhones, a bottle of hand lotion, a pencil sharpener and dozens of other gadgets and accessories.

None of them were there in my village.

How about in the kitchen? The refrigerator, the oven, the stove, the slow cooker, the sink, the toaster, the microwave, the can opener, the juicer, the dining room table, the ceramic cups, the plates, and hundreds of other steel and plastic utensils and gadgets. Our kitchen cabinets are full of stuff that we have stored for years and use once in a while.

None of this was present in our village kitchen.

And did I mention that no one in the village had any idea about what a garage is?

Nayan, though it may be hard for you to fully grasp, I

want you to appreciate my journey. I started in a remote village in a cow-drawn cart and ended up in a carrier, building aircraft. I hope you can see my tenacity and my desire to understand life and overcome every obstacle. Just think, if I hadn't gone to school or engineering college, I couldn't have survived in India. I couldn't have come here and had a wonderful life.

As I've grown, I've begun to realize the great sacrifices my father has made for his children. He was willing to give his life for his kids. The extent of their sacrifice is difficult for even me to understand. Sitting here today in America, I often think, "I'll never be able to do that for my kids."

But what I can do is sacrifice my time and resources to leave this legacy in written form, so that you and the generations to come can learn.

Let the adventure begin.

GLOSSARY OF BENGALI AND BRITISH WORDS

Ashtaprahar celebration —Eight hours of continuous chanting

Babu—Sir

Betan—stick used by policemen

Chamar—a whisk made of cow tails.

Dada / Da—Elder Brother, also referring to a local leader who sometimes extorted money from people in the area, but also protected them from the government and outsiders

Didi / Di—Elder Sister

Dom—funeral attendants who aided with cremation, who belonged to a lower untouchable class because of their occupation

Ghatak—middleman for an arranged marriage

Ghat—steps leading down into a river or pond, often through a terrace

Godown—a warehouse or storage shed.

Hookah—a specialized contraption for vaporizing tobacco.

Jathamosai / Jatha—Father's elder brother

Jathima / Jethi—Jatha's wife

Kaka / Kaku—Father's younger brother

Kakima—Kaka's wife

Kolke—the top portion of a hookah.

Mama—Mother's brother

Mamima / Mami—Mama's wife

Mashi—Mother's sister

Mesomosai / Mesho—Mashi's husband

Mosai—Sir

Outhouse—an outbuilding used as a social gathering place, like a summer house.

Pishemosai / Pishe—Pishi's husband

Pishi—Father's sister

Sri Krishna Chaityana, Prabhu Nityananda, Hare Krishna hare Ram Shree Radhe Gobinda—Usual vaisnav chant.

AUTHOR BIO

Robin Podder was born in 1939 in a remote village in Bangladesh, then a part of undivided British India. His life in the village was almost primitive. There was no electricity, gas, running water, paved road, or transportation except bullock carts.

In 1946 came the communal riot, and in 1947 the end of the British raj, the partition, and the independence. His village fell under the newly created Pakistan. Being Hindu, his family had to leave the village's birthplace and move to Kolkata, India. He got through high school, and college and received his Mechanical Engineering degree (BSME) from Calcutta University in 1960.

In 1975, he immigrated to the USA and naturalized as a US citizen. He got his Master's degree in Mechanical Engineering (MSME) from California State University, Los

Angeles. He held a manufacturing management position at Northrop Grumman Corporation and retired in 1995.

After retirement, he attended the Film School at UCLA. He wrote, directed, and produced an award-winning feature film, "Storm in the Afternoon". He was also hired to direct a second feature, "The Chosen Few".

His memoir UPROOTED is his first nonfiction venture.

robinpodder@gmail.com

BIBLIOGRAPHY AND NOTES

5. Stories After Dark

1. "Churel," *Wikipedia,* Accessed January 18, 2023, https://en.wikipedia.org/wiki/Churel
2. "Ramayana," *Wikipedia,* Accessed January, https://en.wikipedia.org/wiki/Ramayana
3. "Hinduism: Story of Rama and Sita," *Twinkl,* Last modified January 27, 2023, Accessed January 30, 2023, https://www.twinkl.co.uk/homework-help/religion-homework-help/hinduism-facts-for-kids/hinduism-story-of-rama-and-sita
4. "Hinduism: Story of Rama and Sita," *Twinkl,* Last modified January 27, 2023, Accessed January 30, 2023, https://www.twinkl.co.uk/homework-help/religion-homework-help/hinduism-facts-for-kids/hinduism-story-of-rama-and-sita

6. Changing Seasons

1. "The Jute Industry in India," Youtube Video, https://www.youtube.com/watch?v=PAIPFM9O-fM&ab_channel=TheHindu

9. World War II

1. "Bengal famine of 1943," *Britannica,* Accessed January 30, 2023, https://www.britannica.com/topic/Bengal-famine-of-1943
2. "Bengal famine of 1943," *Britannica,* Accessed January 30, 2023, https://www.britannica.com/topic/Bengal-famine-of-1943

10. The Wonders of Kolkata

1. "Phaeton," *Wikipedia,* Accessed January 24, 2023, https://en.wikipedia.org/wiki/Phaeton_(carriage)
2. "Phaeton," *Wikipedia,* Accessed January 24, 2023, https://en.wikipedia.org/wiki/Phaeton_(carriage)

11. Human Madness

1. "THE CALCUTTA RIOTS OF 1946," *Sciences Po,* Accessed January 30, 2023, https://www.sciencespo.fr/mass-violence-war-massacre-resistance/fr/document/calcutta-riots-1946.html.
2. "Direct Action Day," *Wikipedia,* Accessed January 30, 2023, https://en.wikipedia.org/wiki/Direct_Action_Day
3. "Direct Action Day," *Wikipedia,* Accessed January 30, 2023, https://en.wikipedia.org/wiki/Direct_Action_Day
4. "Direct Action Day," *Wikipedia,* Accessed January 30, 2023, https://en.wikipedia.org/wiki/Direct_Action_Day
5. "Direct Action Day," *Wikipedia,* Accessed January 30, 2023, https://en.wikipedia.org/wiki/Direct_Action_Day
6. "Direct Action Day," *Wikipedia,* Accessed January 30, 2023, https://en.wikipedia.org/wiki/Direct_Action_Day
7. "THE CALCUTTA RIOTS OF 1946," *Sciences Po,* Accessed January 30, 2023, https://www.sciencespo.fr/mass-violence-war-massacre-resistance/fr/document/calcutta-riots-1946.html.
8. "THE CALCUTTA RIOTS OF 1946," *Sciences Po,* Accessed January 30, 2023, https://www.sciencespo.fr/mass-violence-war-massacre-resistance/fr/document/calcutta-riots-1946.html.

12. Broken India

1. "Political views of Subhas Chandra Bose," *Wikipedia,* Accessed January 30, 2023, https://en.wikipedia.org/wiki/Political_views_of_Subhas_Chandra_Bose
2. "Political views of Subhas Chandra Bose," *Wikipedia,* Accessed January 30, 2023, https://en.wikipedia.org/wiki/Political_views_of_Subhas_Chandra_Bose

3. Nish Acharya, "Mahatma Gandhi At 150: Lessons On Leadership," Last modified October 2, 2019, Accessed January 30, 2023, https://www.forbes.com/sites/nishacharya/2019/10/02/mahatma-gandhi-at-150-lessons-on-leadership/?sh=35b015d0d7c1

4. "Gandhi begins fast in protest of caste separation," Accessed January 30, 2023, https://www.history.com/this-day-in-history/gandhi-begins-fast-in-protest-of-caste-separation

5. "THE CALCUTTA RIOTS OF 1946," *Sciences Po,* Accessed January 30, 2023, https://www.sciencespo.fr/mass-violence-war-massacre-resistance/fr/document/calcutta-riots-1946.html.

6. "THE CALCUTTA RIOTS OF 1946," *Sciences Po,* Accessed January 30, 2023, https://www.sciencespo.fr/mass-violence-war-massacre-resistance/fr/document/calcutta-riots-1946.html.

7. Pritika Chowdhry, "Partition of India and the dark history of the Radcliffe Line," July 6, 2022, Accessed January 27, 2023, https://www.pritikachowdhry.com/post/partition-of-india-radcliffe-line

8. Pritika Chowdhry, "Partition of India and the dark history of the Radcliffe Line," July 6, 2022, Accessed January 27, 2023, https://www.pritikachowdhry.com/post/partition-of-india-radcliffe-line

9. Pritika Chowdhry, "Partition of India and the dark history of the Radcliffe Line," July 6, 2022, Accessed January 27, 2023, https://www.pritikachowdhry.com/post/partition-of-india-radcliffe-line

10. Pritika Chowdhry, "Partition of India and the dark history of the Radcliffe Line," July 6, 2022, Accessed January 27, 2023, https://www.pritikachowdhry.com/post/partition-of-india-radcliffe-line

11. "Partition and Forced Migrations," Accessed January 30, 2023, https://www.pritikachowdhry.com/silent-waters

12. Jawaharlal, "HOW DID PARTITION CHANGE THE RELIGIOUS MAP IN BENGAL?" *South Asia Blog,* Accessed January 30, 2023, https://southasiablog.wordpress.com/2014/01/23/how-did-partition-change-the-religious-map-in-bengal/

15. A Misadventure

1. "Sonagachi," *Wikipedia,* Accessed January 30, 2023, https://en.wikipedia.org/wiki/Sonagachi

2. "International Photography Awards," Facebook, Accessed January 30, 2023, https://www.facebook.com/photoawards/photos/a.131145703575444/1145623188794352/?type=3

3. "International Photography Awards," Facebook, Accessed January 30, 2023, https://www.facebook.com/photoawards/photos/a.131145703575444/1145623188794352/?type=3

16. Dreaming of Utopia

1. "THE CALCUTTA RIOTS OF 1946," Sciences Po, Accessed January 30, 2023, https://www.sciencespo.fr/mass-violence-war-massacre-resistance/fr/document/calcutta-riots-1946.html

17. Change Agent

1. "Nala (Ramayana)," *Wikipedia,* Accessed January 30, 2023, https://en.wikipedia.org/wiki/Nala_(Ramayana)

19. Getting Married

1. "Bhang Lassi - The Oldest Cannabis Drink From India," *Cannabis Drinks Expo,* February 20, 2020, Accessed January 30, 2023, https://cannabisdrinksexpo.com/en/blog/insights-68/bhang-lassi-the-oldest-cannabis-drink-from-india-187.htm
2. "Bhang Lassi - The Oldest Cannabis Drink From India," *Cannabis Drinks Expo,* February 20, 2020, Accessed January 30, 2023, https://cannabisdrinksexpo.com/en/blog/insights-68/bhang-lassi-the-oldest-cannabis-drink-from-india-187.htm

20. Facing Turmoil

1. M Rajivlochan, "50 years of Naxalite movement: What happened at Naxalbari on May 25, 1967?," Last modified May 25, 2017, Accessed January 30, 2023, https://www.dailyo.in/politics/naxalite-naxalbari-may-25-1967-charu-mazumdar-kanu-sanyal-17404
2. "What is Naxalbari? All you need to know before new Zee5 series drops," Last modified November 25, 2020, Accessed January 30, 2023, https://www.indiatoday.in/binge-watch/story/what-is-naxalbari-all-you-need-to-know-before-new-zee5-series-drops-1743953-2020-11-25

3. Information in this section taken from M Rajivlochan, "50 years of Naxalite movement: What happened at Naxalbari on May 25, 1967?," Last modified May 25, 2017, Accessed January 30, 2023, https://www.dailyo.in/politics/naxalite-naxalbari-may-25-1967-charu-mazumdar-kanu-sanyal-17404